Of Earth and Sea

CAMINO DEL SOL

A Latina and Latino Literary Series

∴   ∴   ∴

Of Earth and Sea

A Chilean Memoir

Marjorie Agosín
translated by Roberta Gordenstein

The University of Arizona Press
Tucson

The University of Arizona Press
© 2009 Marjorie Agosín
All rights reserved

www.uapress.arizona.edu

Interior drawings by Natalia Nakazawa

Library of Congress Cataloging-in-Publication Data

Agosín, Marjorie.
Of earth and sea : a Chilean memoir / Marjorie Agosín ;
translated by Roberta Gordenstein.
p. cm. — (Camino del sol)
ISBN 978-0-8165-2665-9 (hardcover : alk. paper) —
ISBN 978-0-8165-2666-6 (pbk. : alk. paper)
1. Agosín, Marjorie—Anecdotes. 2. Chile—Social life
and customs—20th century—Anecdotes. 3. Chile—
Description and travel. I. Gordenstein, Roberta. II. Title.
F3101.A38A3   2009
983.06'5092—dc22
[B]   2008033643

Publication of this book is made possible in part by the proceeds of a
permanent endowment created with the assistance of a Challenge Grant
from the National Endowment for the Humanities, a federal agency.

14 13 12 11 10 09   6 5 4 3 2 1

Contents

PART II. THE TIMES OF DARKNESS

Translator's Preface

Marjorie Agosín has been writing this book in her head ever since the Chilean coup on September 11, 1973. For seventeen years after Augusto Pinochet took over La Moneda, the presidential palace where Salvador Allende took his last breaths, Chileans experienced life under a regime where those who questioned its legitimacy disappeared, were tortured, and executed. *Of Earth and Sea: A Chilean Memoir* is Agosín's tribute to those who died and those who fought so their country would be free again.

This powerful and poignant collection explores and recreates three important aspects of this distant land. Agosín explores personal and familial history through miniature portraits that reveal the pain of difference, as she revisits her mother's birthplace, a small community of German immigrants, many of them members of the Nazi party who continued to discriminate against the few Jewish families who settled there. In that small town, her mother was an outsider, a Jew, member of a tiny minority. Here she experienced prejudice and cruelty but never lost faith in humanity. We see the racial injustice and anti-Semitism of natives and immigrants alike, as the Jewish children were not permitted to attend either the British or the German schools but were considered as undesirable as the impoverished indigenous population.

Another focus of the book is the physical beauty of this long and narrow nation, surrounded by the vast Pacific Ocean to the south and west and the imposing ice- and snow-covered Andes to the east. *Of Earth and Sea: A Chilean Memoir* evokes the grandeur of a land at the southernmost tip of the world that encompasses desert, ocean, and cordillera. Through her love for her country, Agosín conveys the agony of being in exile, forced by circumstances to leave her home and live as a stranger in countries where her language is often unappreciated. "In exile I fled from the night. . . . I returned to closed rooms, silenced hotels, the silence of strangers in rooms without a balcony, without memory. Then in order to sleep I would conjure up the arrival of night and dream about the stars of the Southern Hemisphere or simply devote myself to holding a conversation with God."

Finally, Agosín introduces us to the great writers and artists of Chile, the Nobel Prize–winning poets Pablo Neruda and Gabriela Mistral, her literary inspirations. We read of the courage of Victor Jara, Violeta Parra, and Charles Horman, all supporters of human rights in Chile, who perished at the hands of the military. We also mourn for the multitude of children and young people who died as a result of Pinochet's cruelty. Meanwhile, their mothers and families demonstrated for them, never losing hope, and demanded their return. Through her writing, Marjorie Agosín conveys their strength and passion.

Of Earth and Sea: A Chilean Memoir reveals Agosín's quest for a home, her own identity and the recreation of memory and the places she loves. The book is a gift to the entire country of Chile, a land that has finally won its struggle for social justice and achieved a true democracy. This volume is filled with compassion and love, and goes beyond the inspiring story of one particular nation to become the greater story of the human condition, where the experience of a particular village transcends the local and approaches the universal. This collection is a book of travels, of journeys not only physical but mental also, through time, space, and memory. *Of Earth and Sea: A Chilean Memoir* is a book about hope, reflecting the landscape of memory. Agosín revisits the memory of the disappeared to make them live again and recalls the history of her land through its painful transition to democracy. With an extraordinarily rich prose, *Of Earth and Sea: A Chilean Memoir* is a culmination of Agosín's dialogue with her homeland.

Roberta Gordenstein
Elms College

Of Earth and Sea

Of Earth and Sea

A Chilean Memoir

I try to speak now of memory, to dialogue with it and assure myself of the precision or imprecision of certain dates, and nevertheless, I realize that even as I muse about memory, there is a tremendous component of pain and forgetfulness. I come from a people with long memories, wanderers, the Jews. The sacred writings, like the Talmud, say that remembering is also a sense of belonging and obligation.

When I began to write *Of Earth and Sea: A Chilean Memoir,* I wanted to describe its marvelous geography, its indescribable beauty, and to tell a brief autobiographical story. The reader will see that in these pages the place named Chile privileges the very lives of the beings who populate its sites, and that the background of this memoir is a land that is generous and dazzling, but more than anything, a land of refugees.

I come from a family of nomads, of immigrants who fled the Holocaust as well as the pogroms of Eastern Europe. Part of this family that survived by chance arrived in Chile around 1920. The first was my grandfather, Joseph Halpern, who later, through tremendous effort, managed to save the life of my great-grandmother Helena and take refuge from the madness of Europe here at the end of the world. My paternal grandparents arrived around 1911 and lived in a small town in the central valley of the country, where they prospered in the happiness of lives free from persecution and danger.

My own life has been spent in many places—the most powerful of these my own imagination—and also in the imagination of my grandparents who told me of their odysseys. I learned to tell stories by listening to them, and I spent my earliest childhood between Santiago and Osorno, and sometimes Valparaíso. I am now fifty-two years old and have tried to relate with the clarity and obscurity of memory my recollections of Chile: the Chile of my childhood with my grandparents in the sixties, and later the Chile of the dictatorship and terror, as well as the Chile of hope and the possibility of living in a democracy.

I recount here the pain and sorrow of my friends and family as they experienced the immediate effects of the coup. From afar I felt their suffering and agony, wishing there was something I could do to show my solidarity with them. I remembered how I felt when my father's books were burned, how helpless we all were. When I was able to return late in 1973, I saw firsthand the destruction and devastation the coup brought upon the Chilean people.

Of Earth and Sea: A Chilean Memoir tells stories both large and small; it speaks of the immensity of a landscape of islands and oceans, of the lives of immigrants, refugees in the thirties, and the life of a young immigrant to America. The chronology at times may be vague, but the major events of the history of the twentieth century, with its disastrous wars as well as its victories, and the beginning of the twenty-first century, are here in its pages.

This book begins in the forties, where I recreate not necessarily the memory I experienced, but rather a memory mediated by the voice of my mother; then it travels to the seventies and speaks of my own memory, memory of the exile of a generation of the disappeared, a generation dispersed.

Of Earth and Sea: A Chilean Memoir arranges history according to a poetic intelligence dominated by the essence of moments, fragments, traces, by the avatars of history. The funeral of Pablo Neruda takes place alongside the lament of women who desperately seek their disappeared sons and daughters. Also permeating this text is the astonishing geography of the country, a geography of rivers, valleys, and desolate landscapes, just as the wind of Patagonia figures prominently with its distant voice, its prophetic voice, its voice that is filled and even overflowing with stories. . . .

Each one of these collages, segments, vignettes should be read like little signs, omens, and secret incrustations, footprints that memory continues to leave. The reader suddenly comes face-to-face with a Patagonian landscape, the beautiful and healing araucaria plant dreaming of summer in the mountains, the widows of Calama caressing the sands of the desert where the remains of their disappeared children sleep.

With its scraps and threads of memory, this book is the history of my country, my years of exile, my returns, but at the same time it represents the voices of an entire generation that deeply loved the possibility of a dream, justice, the transformation of life—a generation that allied itself with the right to claim happiness, to build homes for the peasants, to demonstrate for rights, to study. *Of Earth and Sea: A Chilean Memoir* is their story, and so our own.

More than thirty years have passed since the military coup in Chile, and it seems it was only yesterday that Salvador Allende stood, dignified, in a palace in flames and said that someday we would all walk freely along the immense avenues. Now a woman president traces a new journey in the land of rain and hope, now in a true democracy and with a socialist government it is necessary to stop, to rewrite memory, to rethink the history of this land of rain.

❖ Part I ❖
The Early Years of Childhood: 1960s

Prelude I

My Country

My country is like an undulating streamer. It is the color of earthly objects. I always imagine it as ocher, but all of Chile is very blue, like those cupolas that appear in photographs of colonial churches. I like to go into the churches. I do it secretly, not because my parents forbid me but because here everyone knows I am a Jew. I am only ten, but once a child younger than I spat in my face, and I realized the scope of the hatred that starts like a tiny bush and grows in a crazy and disorderly fashion. The churches are always chilly, and I like to rest my cheek on their limestone walls.

Today is November 1, Día de Todos los Santos, the Day of the Dead. We do not celebrate this holiday. My grandmother says she doesn't know where her dead lie; they are everywhere and therefore she makes it a habit to scatter seeds on the ground so they will have flowers in every season. Spring is beginning to parade radiantly through the meadows, and all the flower stands are filled with gladioli, white lilies, and forget-me-nots. People start to crowd the train stations in order to travel throughout the country and visit their dead. This seems beautiful to me, feeling that they are going to visit the dead, bring them wreaths or their favorite foods. Mama with her brutal honesty tells us that no one comes to our house, not the living or the dead. I like to hear her say all these things. Mama thinks and speaks. She is not moderate in her speech. She even says the Christians are happier than we Jews.

My brother and I approach the plaza where everything and nothing happens. Everyone is dressed in holiday outfits. They are carrying fresh bread, and everywhere there is a smell of rotting flowers. There are enormous lines in the cemeteries, and everyone is waiting for the gates to be opened so they can eat with their dead. People at neighboring graves greet one another.

I gaze at all this with happiness and hope. Sometimes I would like to be Christian, in order to visit the dead, to look at everything so innocently and wear a red dress. But my dead, where are they? At home I start to question everyone about this and sense the fragility of my genealogical tree.

Grandmother believes her sisters are alive, and I wonder why the Jews suffer so much. What have we done to deserve so many defeats? But my father says it is those defeats that frame our faith.

How do you love a country? By sensing its textures from childhood when you traverse its paths and discover its sands, its enormous and generous horizons? How do you speak of a land called Chile, with a geography that shivers because its beauty goes beyond all words? I learned to love Chile through the stories of others, those immigrants who, seated at their humble tables, recounted their emotions when their eyes rested on this country for the first time, and how this land extended its generosity to them.

My nanny Carmen Carrasco taught me to believe in the magic of night and in Saint John's Eve in particular. Women weave and create objects that are beautiful in their simplicity, like the women who always sit at the edges of the road, and from their hands beautiful wooden flowers emerge. Whenever I see them, I cannot help marveling at their work, and I buy armfuls of their colored flowers to carry with me on all my journeys.

Later, I learned to love Chile through its people—Pablo Neruda, Gabriela Mistral, and the indomitable traveler, Maria Graham, an Englishwoman whose husband, a ship captain, was lost at sea, and who settled in Chile and wrote *Diary of My Residence in Chile*. Through them I imagined every part of this land.

Now, motivated by a moment of grace, a grace like love, I write about my country and its spaces, about silent Patagonia, Isla Negra, and about its people, the women of Pomaire. I tell of certain regions and certain people who managed to forge a divine moment in my soul, a story to recount so the reader may discover with the same passion as I this extensive and perplexing land named Chile.

Imagine, then, a land long and restless like the dream of a girl who wishes to be a pixie or a princess. Imagine a land with eight hundred volcanoes that blink like rainbows playing with a gilded and diaphanous time. Imagine a land with a poet who is ocean, mountain range, and wind. A poet named Chile, a Chile named Neruda. Imagine snow-capped mountains and blue glaciers. Imagine a teacher-poet, a wanderer who is also named Gabriela Chile and a Chile named Gabriela.

Santiago is my city; it is there where I find myself and lose myself, where I dream and suffer from insomnia. It is the city of my first kiss and my first poems about it. My memories are of frost-covered mornings, the grass like a single sliver of ice, the midday sun, Carmen Carrasco, who watched over my first steps, and so many other things, like the first snow over the city, falling like gentle, crystalline drops, adorning the homes of rich and poor alike. Drops of snow, light as the first dream of a child.

My friend Marisa Fried lives in a house where a tree grows among the thresholds. She complains about this tree, because lovebirds nest there and eat the blackberries of the savory summertime, but I am thrilled to know that in these huge old homes of Santiago, trees still rule the lives of the residents, and birds find a place that will accommodate their lovemaking.

Marisa sweeps away what the birds leave behind, sings in the city of Santiago where the trees sink their roots between the beds. And in their lofty crowns, they let the wind hide secrets and seeds.

You always have to look at the magnificent Andes to know exactly where you are in the city of Santiago, and they will show the true routes and the imaginary ones. At dawn you greet them, lifting your gaze toward them; you feel insignificant facing their plenitude, but at the same time you know you belong to them, just like the snow that slides through their skirts of ice.

From these latitudes and longitudes, from the archipelagoes that break loose like skeins of sun and bunches of grapes, I came to name objects with the humility of those blessed by miracles, of the astonished, and I became a child who dreams and an old woman who dreams. And from that land I learned the alphabet of precarious things, the ineffable time of poetry that is the time of history.

In Osorno, My Mother's City

My country is surrounded by an endless sea and encircled by mountains. It would seem to be protected from every evil, but still, in the south of Chile, in the little town of Osorno, lived the Nazis. They found a refuge here just like my grandparents, who had recently arrived from a Europe burnt to ashes. My mother lived in Osorno, near the 40th parallel, at the very end of the earth, from the thirties until the forties, when she left with my grandparents for Santiago, a city that offered greater opportunities to exist and grow. The powerful Nazi presence in the south even after the war made this transplantation necessary. But she always told me stories of its streets, its secrets, her house of light wood that seemed to see the entire world through its windows. My mother lived there through adolescence and then moved to Santiago, where she fell in love and had her children.

In Santiago we could breathe more freely, and my mother told me that on the day the Second World War ended, residents of Santiago went out to the streets throwing rose petals. I think it was at that moment that Santiago became a part of us. My life in Santiago passed in a house filled with windows and gardens that looked only toward the back. Here I went to school and learned to read and sing on my father's lap.

I am from Santiago but I am also an itinerant wanderer, traveling between the north and south of my land. My mother would tell me stories of nights when the moon seemed like a very long beard, and she learned to name the stars. One day she told me about her experiences at school. I preserved her story; sometimes I feel it is my own. As a child, at the end of the fifties, I returned often to Osorno and visited Port Octay, and the memories my mother recalled remained engraved in my imagination. For me, Osorno was both a real city and another that existed in my mother's mind. I learned to love the southern part of my country, with its volcanoes that illuminate my fearful dreams at night.

In September of 1972, at sixteen, I left Chile for North America, where I had to learn another language. We left behind us a huge family of grandparents, aunts and uncles, and cousins. My grandparents remained there until the end of their lives. They are buried in the Jewish cemetery in Valparaíso. I always felt they were taking care of the country. It was through them I learned of those who disappeared, those who could not be forgotten. My memory lived through years of long letters and journeys home. It seemed I was living in two pieces: in the mornings I spoke English, and at night I dreamed in Spanish. Unlike many others, I was able to return, and when I did, I devoted myself to recording what I saw from the outside.

We made that painful journey of immigration alone. Even today my immediate family lives in North America. My mother still lives in Athens, Georgia, where we settled. I married a North American, and my two children still speak the language of my childhood that provided me with a sense of permanence and feeling. We continue to gaze at the Southern Hemisphere, at that distant land that offered hope and refuge to my family fleeing the Holocaust. Among them was my great-grandmother Helena, who reached the coast of Valparaíso on a cargo ship in 1938. My mother tells me how they went out to greet her and describes her beautiful silk gloves and the garnet ring I hold today in my hands, reminding me of the courage of all journeys and the comfort Chile offered us.

I realize that when Mama talks about Osorno her voice is in two continents—first, that of the leveled and lost Europe she never knew and that Josefina, her mother, used to tell her about, and the second, South America. At night, unable to sleep and bewildered by obsessive memory, she stops to gaze at the Chilean sky beyond the Three Marys and wonders about the living and the dead, remembering a past she has only heard about.

My grandparents and my mother lived in Osorno during the Second World War, between 1938 and 1944. Even though for many that war was distant, since it took place in Europe and not in South America, I think it was impossible not to know about it, not to experience it or hear it constantly on the radio in southern Chile, despite that Chile was so far removed from the sites of the war, despite that so many Chileans were fervent Nazi supporters. In this house it was possible to listen to European radio that informed them regularly of the war. My mother said my grandmother sketched a map and marked the triumphs of the Allies on it with colored ribbons. The experience of the Second World War in Chile takes on other shades that often pass unnoticed. During the Second World War, the collective memory of Chile became ambiguous and devoid of anything having to do with truth.

My mother grew up in the south of Chile in a town of transplanted Germans, a few Chileans, and a handful of Jews. She lived there secluded behind the thresholds, hearing words in other languages, spoken by a grandmother dreaming of her murdered cousins. I too went to that house in Osorno among the forests and the ibises, and at times I dreamed I had grown up there too, but these were the stories Mama told me that came to live in my memory.

Chile maintained a powerful neutrality during the years of the war. That is to say, it maintained relations with Germany, and in the region where Mama lived, the powerful German influence remained intact. It is hard to talk about the war and the Nazis in Chile. The memory of my country, or what I imagine my country was, seems to become diluted. History is condemned or condensed to certain moments of nobility. Although they celebrated with equal happiness battles lost and won as if they were all great accomplishments, it was not so long ago that the Nazis were the feudal lords of southern Chile and the few Jewish families watched with sadness the passing of the seasons, as if they were only transitory guests on the earth.

Mama told me that in Osorno she was afraid, but this fear was inexplicable and alien. It was a fear that had to do with incomprehensible things, things lost in vain. Fear seethed through the nights as if it were a ghost on an abandoned ship. Mama said there was no possible hiding place, and she would place her ears next to the cold walls of the house to assure herself that life continued in its full and never-ending rhythm.

Life in Osorno transpired at a slow pace. Days seemed to follow a constant routine marked by the clear passing of time, by the always-fleeting light that seemed to waver on days of rain. Everything in Osorno was shielded, concealed, and my mother lived a life in two versions, in two universes, hearing German in her father's voice and, at the same time, in the mouths of the girls from the German school, where they were forbidden to speak Spanish.

We hesitate before the memory of certain cities. We want to be sure of how they are remembered. Sometimes when my mother and I would devote ourselves to stretching out on our backs and feeling the leisure of hours of relaxation that crackled over our skin, we would long to be two speedy lizards taking pleasure in the creaking wood. Then I would ask Mama to tell me stories, to recall her city, because Osorno, in spite of everything, was her city, the one she would imagine during moments of happiness and refuge. She said that in her room in the attic, there was an enormous round window like a skylight, where she used to gaze at the passing of the ibises. Nature was lush and prominent. Life in Osorno was intimately joined to the passing of time, the larch trees, the roaring of life and the winds. That's the way things were. Questions arose only when there was nothing to ask about, and nothing to discuss or not discuss.

Mama always said that in Osorno she learned the secret and mystery of herbs and the possibilities they offered, and she learned secrets that would cure the sorrows of the soul as well as everyday ills, such as indigestion. I too learned the secret of herbs from her, what was necessary to cure fright, anxiety, and fear.

The women who sold herbs seemed to travel barefoot through the city. It was not even possible to hear their sounds on the cobblestones, only their voices. I have always managed to associate the voices of these women with the voices of a fragrance that appeared before any physical presence. That is to say, the fragrances presupposed stories that could be seen, heard, and felt; they seethed untamed among the herbs or could be heard crackling like the nights of fire that remained tattooed in all our memories. Mama taught me about these fragrances, the ones that reach us as if they were the wild beating of wings or the most precious memories.

Where did the centuries, the stories, the sounds of day and the sounds of night go? The first story I learned from her was about the poppies. Mama always sang a song called, "Poppy, Sweet Poppy," and I imagined her with this flower occupying the most sacred spot in her heart. Later I learned that when she was a child, they would give her poppy-scented water to drink to calm her nerves. Now they extract the elixir for opium from this luminous flower.

Mama told what was necessary about those years, but perhaps something in that landscape transformed her into what she was and what she continues to be, a girl who seemed like a puff of wind, a girl sunken in a melancholy and silence that could not be heard, that seemed to become dislodged and break off, to emerge from the most intense part of language.

I learned more about those days from what she did not say than from what she did, from the spaces Mama allowed to be inhabited or not inhabited. And in that way I too continued weaving little stories about southern Chile. Perhaps certain places do not deserve to be mentioned, while others do in order to enter them and reveal enigmas, to sense the strangeness of the times.

In spite of our exile during the reign of Pinochet, I traveled all those years and lived between two countries, two cultures, two histories. But the land of rain, the land surrounded by water and mountains, has remained inscribed on my skin and in my memory.

My Mother

In our house in Santiago my mother is always on the lookout for the first stars. The sky is so blue, a cobalt blue, a blue the color of the sea. My mother wears a pashmina shawl that covers her shoulders, and to me she looks like an angel at rest. She tells me she sees in every star the faces of her family members who are gone, and she names them as if she were shelling peas and beans. When she names them, her eyes light up and are extinguished like two fireflies.

I always thought my mother would fit in my hands; she is still small and light, like the light her eyes reveal. I pictured her as small because I looked at the world from the dimension of my own height. Our childhood was shared, she and I, the two of us, like abandoned children facing the invisible things in life: seashells, stars, the sounds of imaginary animals. At night she would tell me stories, adventures of disobedient young girls, and sometimes, on rare occasions, she would tell me of her distant childhood at the south of the world, in the south of Chile, in Osorno, where she spent her earliest years. It was a time of disasters, she says, and of wars, more or less around the year 1939, when Europe was aflame and she, that little girl, my mother, knew they had murdered her family.

We hardly spoke of that at home, and we lived with our ghosts, our dead, forever abiding with them, never abandoning them to the remoteness of oblivion.

Most of my childhood passed in the city of Santiago, with occasional visits to the south. My mother belonged to the forests, the frozen landscapes, the small streams; I grew up between the mountain ranges and the sea, protected by those two immense entities that allowed me to dream.

The House at the Southern Tip of the World

The house at the southern tip of the world was always open. It awakened in the morning to welcome the women who walked through dense and frost-covered meadows until they reached the homes of the city-dwellers, where they offered their freshly made bread and their hands that were born knowing the rhythm of the dough. They arrived carrying straw baskets, wearing white aprons, and in my child's eyes they were the brides of the morning. The women who sold violets also came from their villages at twilight with faded blossoms they brought to exchange for a small piece of stale bread or tea with lime-tree leaves. My mother welcomed them all. She liked to chat with them, and I think that far from the hateful hierarchies, she felt more at home surrounded by them and their fresh and fading fragrances.

On Fridays, my grandmother said that the world should rest, that was what God commanded: letting oneself be carried away by the hours, understanding time as a circular course. I opened the door to those who had lost keys, homes, tablecloths, or their loved ones of whom we were not allowed to speak.

Then we would light the Friday-night candles, and night would fall, cool and simple over the dinner-table conversation. Many people said, "I have no money to pay for this meal, but I can offer you this song." Each one remembered with his voice his beloved languages, his cities of fire and wrath. Song lightened their souls, and music was a tattooed memory.

That is what our Fridays were like in this house at the southern tip of the world, where the overflowing wind devoted itself to hearing uncertain voyagers who had found refuge in this desolate country in the middle of an almost unimaginable remoteness.

Ramírez Street

Every Saturday we like to chat as we take a walk along Ramírez Street. Mama says that elegance lies in simplicity. She does not like the women with long eyelashes and reddish hair. The truth is, we do not have a lot of clothing, and every Saturday Carmen irons my white blouse and my pleated skirt that looks like a giant accordion. Mama wears her sable stole, strange pieces of fur with the little animal faces that she drapes around her neck as if they were a great scarf. Mama walks erect and pays her respects. I play, whistle, sing, and collect chestnuts. Life is an extraordinary adventure for me, and the street is a delight of sounds and possibilities. Here on these Saturday excursions, I learn an infinite number of secrets; for example, to cure lovesickness you must drink artemisia tea, and to alleviate menstrual cramps, you must breathe lavender oils.

I like to listen to the herb seller or the woman who bestows violets upon lovers. Gestures of love exist next to those of indifference. There are people who snub one another, others who smile. Unbelievable to me are the quarrels that last more than a hundred years. Our strolls along Ramírez Street make our lives pleasant. You can see widows of the upper aristocracy strolling with their maids, street vendors hawking their merchandise: knives, keys, screws for repairs.

More than anyone else, we notice Mrs. Shripman, always at the door of her shop, who signals to us with her enormous mouthful of gold teeth. All the passersby stop, greet her; the children hide behind their mothers and stare at one another. Mrs. Shripman seems like a lighthouse in the immensity of Ramírez Street.

Sometimes her teeth seem to be a gigantic sunflower that lights the path for us. Other times she is a mysterious force that attracts us to her doors. I wonder what her nights must be like, always embroidered beneath that golden cloak that covers and uncovers them, which encloses them like the wrappers around chocolates.

The history of Mrs. Shripman is as mysterious as her teeth that obsessively light up and are extinguished like festive candles. They say she had a great love affair, and in order to experience desire and the passion of flesh and body, he removed all her teeth that were good and healthy and replaced them with those gold teeth that are like an insatiable crown of brilliant objects.

Jewish New Year in the South of the World

My family had the gift or the curse of being wanderers. The stories of our nomadic adventures formed a large part of our fables. My grandparents recounted their lengthy journeys from Odessa to Istanbul, and then on to Marseilles before eventually disembarking in Chile. Before living many years in Osorno, my family lived in the port city of Valparaíso, a port of refuge and salvation. Since my grandfather spoke only German, he decided to move to the south of Chile, near the lakes and volcanoes that more than anything reminded him of his distant Austria.

Now Grandmother is preparing for the New Year. She says she feels the beating of hope. Spring is beginning to blush. Sometimes I think about love and smile as if I could hear the sound of bells. Grandmother says we should look for green, like the forests of this Araucaria region that gave her shelter. Carmencha arrives with jars of homemade honey, and suddenly Grandmother smiles with a laugh that comes from deep within and says, "Let sweetness reign on earth." People ask her questions about her distant land, and she says her only country is Israel; all other places are only ashes and stories of ashes.

We all sit down on the patio, and on the table are plates of apples, freshly cooked chicken, and the kugel. Traditional European foods are strange here at the end of the world, but there is something in these aromas, in that blue cabbage, that transports us to some distant place, to solitude. We sing throughout the long night. Our bodies become lighter. We are like the breeze, the drizzle, the smells that make us uneasy and carry other stories. Grandmother prays in a language that is no longer strange to any of us, and we all experience the Hebrew alphabet as if it were a single braid that revolves, sings, moans, and dreams.

This night is definitely different from all other nights. It is the beginning, the offering of the first fruits, and the palate is a swarm of sweet words. Grandmother lights her candelabra, and the breath of God settles over the tenuous melody of candles that sing.

Chanukah in Osorno

We celebrate the first night of Chanukah with the Smirnoffs and the Borochecks. I remember that the nights of Chanukah foretold the sparkle of the beginning of summer, the pleasure of certain breezes that caress my whole body. Our friends come on foot. We all live nearby in the oldest neighborhood of the city, near the plaza that has a traffic circle in the middle. On Sundays, the aristocrats of the town stroll by very slowly with their hands clasped behind them. The Jews go out on Friday nights to smell the perfume of the violets and jasmine.

We light the first candle on the menorah that Papa bought on one of his early trips to Santiago. I like this first light, which is always accompanied by melodies and undulating breezes like the breath of God.

We like to be together, singing and chatting in a multitude of languages. Tonight, Papa gives me a cello. It is a very large but elegant instrument. It looks like a fat feudal lady. I had never seen such a thing. I don't know if I will be able to carry it, but Papa says I will be a great cellist one day, like his cousins, whom I never met.

I approach the cello and Papa says he will buy me a special chair so I will be able to play it. Suddenly I see the cello as a very tiny instrument, warm, emerging from a recent dream. I touch it and it emits a very sad and distant sound from its voice of frozen winds. It is a voice that pauses and seems to be the very beginning of things. Mama gazes at us and for the first time I see her cry, saying that Chaim would be happy knowing that I am playing the cello.

That night I take the cello up to my room. I rest my cheek on its heart and understand that this cello had a passion and a history, it had belonged to a loved one. My cello is sumptuous, melancholy, distant, and completely mine, all at the same time.

Churches

For me, churches signified desire, mystery, and the presence of hidden things. On winter days I used to rest my hands in front of the candles that blinked uncertainly as if they were the whistles of pious women or fearful brides. My beloved nanny, Carmen, faithful to her Catholic tradition, would tell me to light candles to remember the dead, to fulfill promises, because souls demand payment, like the devil. I smiled and always lit a candle thinking about Grandmother's sisters. I saw them resting over a forest of poppies, always asleep.

In the summers I would lay my face on the hard stucco walls, and prayer would bring me a pleasure similar to the miraculous desire the body feels when it knows it is so alive.

As a child I tried to go to confession, not only to talk with the priest, but also to know what there was beyond, behind the things in the apex of the mystery that those doors enclosed. I knew that on opening them, I would find neither heaven nor hell, only the voice of a sexton as lost and hopeful about the mystery of God and prayer as I.

There are no synagogues in Osorno. We pray silently in the homes of our friends. God listens and does not listen, my mother says. My grandmother covers her face, so that the light of the Sabbath will dazzle her and us. I surrender myself completely to the mystery; incredulous, I believe like an unbeliever. In the distance the wind is like a scar in the Osorno night at the end of the world, like the rhythm of those who pray as if they dreamed, as if they believed.

Port Octay

Sometimes we go to Port Octay, not far from Osorno, in the afternoons when the trees point out the stony paths. Here legends as well as ghosts wander the streets. The road to Port Octay is winding, and a river in the shape of a young girl's waist surrounds it. Mama gazes toward the horizon. Everything there is a great covered space, where the zones of silence and her gaze are intertwined.

We go to Frida Haase's hotel, established by her father. He was the captain of a ship that was wrecked on its way from some town in Germany; he came to write a new story among the forests and this perpetual rain. My father likes the hotel. He eats his kuchen and chats in German, something that reminds him of his past.

At home we speak only of the living. It is not necessary to talk with the dead who are in the family's living room, watching, waiting, and expecting replies. Frida Haase is a girl made of china who plays the piano. In the doorway of her abandoned hotel, she dreams of a prince who will come to dance with her at dusk. I am afraid of her strangeness, of that hotel where everyone walks around with heads down, and where it is necessary to steady oneself on the walls.

In this hotel I sense death, and from my tender age I understand fleeting things, unsuspecting nights, transitory noises, and things belonging to others. Nothing belongs to us, and perhaps Frida Haase plays the piano like a ghost. In the distance a southerly wind plunges us into a transitory darkness, and the rain silences our steps.

My father gazes into the distance. He does not exist in this place in the world, and I do not know how to call him. The dead signal to us. They have arrived in Port Octay again to search for us.

Snow at the Southern Tip of the World

Grandmother imagines the snow and collects the snow. She tells me it is so white and plentiful that it seems like a deep lake, always at peace. Sometimes it snows in Osorno, and the Germans go out on their skis to parade through the city. We improvise with pieces of wood, old tree trunks, and glide toward a city that also is astonished by its white blanket. We Chileans and Jews are pitifully inept. The Germans laugh at us and call us pigs. That is how I recall my first day of snow.

At night I like to watch my grandmother sleeping. I wonder in what cities she has been, where she rested her body that reminds me now of a lost sailing ship. I see her curl up as if she were a misplaced seashell. That seashell emits soft and intermittent sounds, troubled moans. I come closer to her, and she sleeps like marine algae wrapped in the thickness of her own hair. Grandmother names strange cities, unexpected places, and tangled forests. Startled, she awakens like a solitary seagull.

Gracefulness

My father taught me the joy of gracefulness, and the gracefulness of signs. Little by little, life became the trembling of astonishment, and so I learned to feel the presence of nocturnal butterflies or imagine that a voice like mine might be a firefly. I walk through the southern countryside; the volcanoes of Osorno and Calbuco play at appearing and disappearing without any warning, like laughter, fear, or an unexpected perfume in the woods. And so life appears radiant and splendid to me. My father smiles, my grandmother understands everything in her simple silence.

Perhaps this is a tiny bit of happiness, understanding things without understanding them, and sensing that time is a clear mirror of our days in the middle of an untamed space. My father does not talk about Vienna or the war, and in that refusal to talk, he says it all. Sometimes while he shaves, I hear him whistling Viennese operettas. My grandmother says that ghosts appear within our prayer books, and the housemaids sing the "Ave Maria" all day long, but nothing separates me from this happiness, from the possibility of breathing deeply, sensing, feeling the pulse of the damp earth and the caress of God on objects where a simple glance lingers.

From these morning sighs I could make earrings, from the copihues I might stain my lips crimson. In this region marked by fog and the crosses of neighboring churches and German settlers who sometimes mistake me for one of them, I am happy.

Carmen Carrasco, My Nanny

For Carmen, signs were predictions, messages from angels and devils. She would wrap up her mature, thick body as if it were a magnificent onion that should be peeled slowly, cautiously, but with tremendous gentleness. Sometimes I would accompany her to her room at the end of the house, passing through gloomy corridors, darkened attics. In her room clarity seemed like a sigh, the breath of objects on earth. Carmen Carrasco did not believe in Jesus or in Moses, although she would say that it was better, in order to prevent misfortune, to eat the body of Christ in a crisp little cracker and throw holy water on the forehead of heretics.

She would say all this with pleasure and cunning while she prepared the maté and brandy. I liked her room, because it smelled like enclosure and clarity. The clothes she wore took on an indescribable smell, somewhere between rotten and dusky, the smell of used clothing, but at the same time, of the eucalyptus leaves she always hid under the bed.

Superstitions were not her obsession or her fears, but part of living. She learned from Mama that if you sneeze while talking about the dead, it is a good idea to scratch your nose. There were times when her entire body seemed to be invaded by a tremendous lethargy, as if something were emerging or being exhumed from the bottom of the earth. Carmen would tell me that we should go out to the garden because night was preparing itself for a great opening when the forest would reveal its secrets and the angels would signal us from their cupolas. All of this created a wonderful happiness for me that allowed me to understand things that were unspoken and dreams that would bring textures and astonishment.

Carmen Carrasco was my faithful nanny. She taught me about ambiguity and certainty, about not knowing and the fact that sometimes we are born already knowing things. On nights when we went out into the garden, I saw nothing, or maybe I saw everything, and she told me that soon I would see the procession of the dead, as if they were former guests sitting in the garden. She was careful with her words, but not with the song she sang to frighten away unlucky spirits and soothe her sorrows. Because she always walked around with a hair ribbon tied around her neck, and scarf pins between her thin lips, I sometimes imagined she would swallow those pins while she told us stories, but she said it was a sign of good manners to be sparing in speaking. On the anniversary of her death, I light the white candles she said were the color of paradise, and I hear her again praying the Our Father to protect me from my Jewish heritage.

Perhaps it was from her that I learned that prejudice has more to do with ignorance than with evil, and that people were like Carmen Carrasco, naturally suspicious of strangers and of those who did not wear a Maltese cross.

I can feel her approaching and whispering things in my ear, with her shawl the color of ashes, her apron covered with ginger and jasmine. Carmen taught me many things, especially how to speak with objects, animals, the wind, and her ramshackle sewing machine. She never spoke much about the time of the earthquake in Chillán, and she seemed to be a woman with insomnia, terrified. We could never learn from her what had happened there. She went to the next life keeping secrets, like the one about the day when the earth swallowed up everything and her voice became silenced.

In Chile we remember with nostalgia all the losses, the earthquakes, the storms when the sea whips the homes of the rich and the poor, but the story of the earthquake in Chillán was kept like a dark and hidden gem in a chrysalis torn in the face of grief. Sometimes I wonder if Carmen dreamed of finding her son Victor among the crevices of a terrified city, the way I dream today of finding my friends who disappeared, those who crossed the mountains and were lost in silence on the horizon.

The Servant Girls

The servant girls are the ones who help Carmen shell the peas, bone the chickens, and watch over the tubs of hot water for Saturday-night baths, because it is the custom here at home to bathe only once a week. They do not know how to read. They are ashamed to tell me this, but I know it. Little by little, when confidence is stronger than shame, I sit down with my spelling book and show them how to put words together. I tell them that the letters are friends, that they join together and sing. I see them smile. Their faces are the color of the earth, an ocher tone. They like to sit down with me while I teach them to read. I am going to be two things in my life: a poet and a teacher. Here the old men of the town, those gentlemen who walk around with dark ties and their hands clasped behind them, who walk so pompously through the streets of the town, say that reading is dangerous and the world is terrifying. More terrifying is ignorance, my mother says as she gazes at me with a sweet smile. I decide to conduct my little school primarily on days of loneliness and winter. Now the house is filled with people who talk and laugh. Sometimes when the women are happy, I hear them speaking Mapuche,* which is their own language, always theirs and not ours.

Yesterday, Grandmother began to peel the first vegetables of the harvest. The house was filled with greens, with cilantro and boldo. Everything seemed to be newly born from the heart of the

---

*The indigenous people of southern Chile and Argentina are the Mapuche; also known by the Spanish conquistadors as *Araucanos*, now considered pejorative.

earth, and we placed our hands on the harvest, giving thanks for the intensity of the yield.

Slowly I bend over the table made of light wood that brings us back to our roots. Perhaps my grandmother is thinking about that tree beside Isidoro's grave in the Jewish section of the cemetery. She says she used to talk with that tree, with its shadows and stories. I ask her why the dead must be buried separately according to their religion, and Grandmother caresses the lentils, shells the peas, and in that silence responds.

Gypsies

Mama loves the Gypsy women who came to Chile from Eastern Europe, because of the mystery of their open and transparent hands in the midst of immense human fragility and vulnerability. From childhood she told me that she would gaze at them with a certain envy and desire to be like them, itinerant dreamers, nocturnal dancers through these lands formed with wonder. The Gypsy women fascinate her, with their varicolored skirts and their flashing decks of cards. When Mama was my age, she would sit down to talk with them about their dreams and their daring, and while she sighed gently, they would invent miraculous destinies and fortunes for her. Once they told her she would have a daughter with very light eyes and even lighter skin in the middle of the desert and that she would travel with her in a second-class covered wagon through the pampas and saltpeter works of Chile. One day this daughter would have the gift of words and music.

My mother asked the Gypsies their names in order to thank them for the favor so graciously granted, and they told her that they could reveal only the future of true gifts, and never their names, which they themselves did not know. Mama thought that one of them, the eldest, who wore golden skirts and blouses of violet crepe, was named Hilaria, because it was an ancient name that smelled like olden times and spells.

When Mama says goodbye to them, they kiss like old friends who will never see each other again. The truth is that I was born in the desert in the town of Andacoyo, where a miraculous virgin lives who helps wandering magicians and artists. My skin was light, and my hair even lighter. They called me Saint Hilaria, and my mother, when she heard that name, knew that she had hit the mark when thinking about that wise Gypsy who had given her a fistful of garlic cloves, a red ribbon, and the gift of hope.

Wool

I like to watch how she winds the wool into a ball. The motion is always the same. She repeats the movements and ways in which the skeins are fastened. I arrange my hands so that my nanny can use me as a frame for winding. The women weave and unweave. That is how they spend their lives, that is how they recount their sorrows. I learn to listen to sounds, whispers and lamentations all through the night.

The wool has the smell of country things, the way I imagine the wheat fields. The women do not wear makeup or expensive perfumes. They are simple, like the wheat that always appears fresh and warm in the inn.

My mother gazes distantly at Grandmother, who opens her notebook of dreams and jots down her thoughts in German. Then she lights her silver candlesticks.

In the distance they are singing in Mapuche. Two different worlds live together here. It is strange being from one and not the other.

Refugees

My mother tells me how she accompanied my grandfather* to the train station in 1939. It was a slow and calm summer day. The entire countryside seemed to be submerged in a luminous lethargy, and in the distance you could hear the song of the ibises that foretells the arrival of guests. There was no one in the station when they arrived, only the usual drunk and the madwoman of the town, who asked if they had seen God enter the cantina. They found themselves in that desolate station waiting for the other passengers who were coming to the end of the earth in search of light and refuge. The whistle of the train announced its arrival. It came slowly and tiredly, crossing this country to finally rest in Osorno. My grandfather signaled to them, and when the starving women descended, he presented them with flowers from the countryside, wild and fresh flowers, and he kissed their hands.

Afterward, they went on foot to the house, where my mother's mama waited for them with wild strawberries and an apple strudel. They sat down at the round table, and my grandfather began to speak in German. I knew they were talking about the news of the war.

*Joseph Halpern, originally from Vienna, arrived in Chile around 1920 and fell in love with it. He later sent for his mother and brother, saving them from the horror of Nazism.

The Salamanders

On the steps beyond time and hoarfrost, winter renews its ceremonies of fog. Here in the south of Chile, the forests are felled
by cold. My mother is dressed like a gray child and dreams of
cast-iron salamander stoves.

The fire is mysterious in its dreamlike movements. My grandparents wonder about those who existed once upon a time, while
a child old beyond her years gazes toward the leveled forest and
imagines the genealogy of her truncated family fleeing, naked.

It is raining in the south of the world, in Osorno, where the
few Jews surrounding the salamander question the sinful fire
about the widows, the silent children. And my mother gazes at
the Chilean woods as if she imagines that beyond the horizon her
cousins, her dead grandmothers, would come to her, because she
needs to speak of other memories and other homes.

In this winter I imagine plains, meadows, leveled forests, the
old salamander hissing names.

A Sash of Smoke

Then the road lies behind us like a sash of smoke, the women who signal to us with their straw baskets and their great and small stories. Mama sends us north to the Pacific coast every summer, because she says we will never grow living in these damp southern climates. The first time we traveled to the central region of Chile was when my great-grandmother arrived at the pier of Valparaíso. It was a victorious day, with the splendid colors of days at the coast. Now we are returning once again to the home of my aunt and uncle, who always wait for us at the train station with chocolates and percale fabrics, because Mama wants me to have stylish clothing.

The trip is long, the country extensive and overflowing in the eccentricity of its landscapes. The train is always secure but silent; it moves with the constancy of memory. It articulates the pathways knowingly. It slips away along the peaks of the mountain and descends through violet-colored fields. The color of this land is a delight, but the color of this land is also shaded by smoke, by invisible things, by a sound that seems to point out what is invisible to our eyes.

Slowness demands caution and peace. The train seems to have all the patience in the world, and we, anxious, hold ourselves tightly in front of the immense windows as if each passing landscape might reveal the secrets and stories of its inhabitants to us. There is something that reminds us of the trajectory of remoteness, of stories that are suggestions of other ages. The music of the train puts us to sleep. I move closer to my brother and read comic books to him. Behind us, Carmen in her shawl probes the fate of each one of the travelers.

I like to travel and feel that I do not give to my journey or my story directions or precise moments. Everything is a gray mantle, a vapor in the midst of the woods, a moan like a whisper.

Pomaire

The craftswomen of Chile make magic with their hands, from the potters of Pomaire, to the makers of beautiful little animals at Quinchamalí, to those who weave enormous scarves of colors both real and imaginary. Most of all, I celebrate the artisans of Panimávida who make colorful butterflies out of tenuous threads of horsehair. Today I place them next to my window; from the prodigious hands of these women, I dream all night long of a copper-colored monarch butterfly.

The seafarer reaching Valparaíso always feels the protection of its bays, the certainty of arrival at a warm and welcoming terra firma. Beyond all the horizons, the hills are like dragonflies, like fireflies, like stories clothed in magic. My grandmother tells me stories of love, sometimes she invents them, or else she takes them from the book she keeps in her blue boxes, and it seems that she invents these too, but then she tells me about Atkinson Promenade, where the women dress up and pretend to be young girls strolling about as if they were searching for other times and other stories, just as in every story of love.

Wine Country

From early childhood, when one sees things with daring and uncertainty, I was able to sense and understand, although not entirely, the magic of wine. In regions of my country like the Maipo Valley or Casablanca, grapes grow between the shadows and the slits of the sun. That mysterious humidity lends the wine a silent elegance and a delightfulness that should be savored slowly, the way one discovers a body during lovemaking and caresses it.

At home we drank wine in different ways. On holidays, in holy glasses. They were holy because of the essence of the ritual that accompanied them, that solemnity of the song and prayer over wine. Thus I learned the subtleties of silence and peace that are found in a glass of ancestral and holy wine.

Although wine marks the seasons, and the celebrations of Jewish and Christian rituals, it is also a communal event. It belongs to the heritage of the homeland. In the countryside, on national holidays, we drink fresh *chicha*. From childhood I regarded this drink with a certain suspicion and caution, because it was fermented wine. Later I learned that even in its most basic state, wine holds an honest elegance that comes from the most ancient forms of pleasure.

Throughout the length of our country, grapes are cultivated for wine, and the vineyards carry the names of great aristocratic families or those who little by little dared to cultivate this knowledge that transforms the land, the palate, and desire.

Chile's wines are as varied as its geography. The red wines are passionate and brazen. At first they lighten the palate to later enrich the senses. They bring sweetness to life and time, and as we hold the wine in our hands, it acquires the luminosity of a brave and bold poppy in the vastness of night. Drinking these wines allows us to ride horseback into other histories.

I have seen the arrival of night when old people of the town hold a wake for their dead. From their voices arises a song that comes from the hills, beyond the valleys where time and the horizon cannot be distinguished, and the wine accompanies death and soothes the living.

Summer in Isla Negra

The chores begin in the slowness of an awakening without haste. Time is a game that teaches us to tarry. I like to see things awakening; they are always transparent, and I awaken barefoot, unassuming. The smell of the carnations reaches me, the smell of braided bread, creamy coffee and milk. Always the sense of fragrance first, mint, rosemary, sweet basil, like the saunter of a woman in love.

It is summer, day extends like a golden wing. In the distance I imagine the road, lilac like the color of the trees, the dust from the few cars, the guests who will arrive.

Leisure allows me to imagine poems; the letters dance, the spelling stares at me, alphabets write themselves on my back. Imprecise, irresistible, leisure brings me the freedom to change, dream, imagine. Carmencha calls me, her voice is like the crevices, like the earth that separates and is strung together. She asks me to help her shell the French beans. I take them out of their skins, one by one, my hands and the beans in the monotony of a marvelous rhythm. The hours slip away over a large earthen jar, where the beans fall like waterfalls for the palate. I daydream during lunch. I dream during the siesta, when I imagine myself a sultan, the sea in the distance and ships that disembark magicians, messengers, furtive princes.

I read books about natural history, but nothing equals experiencing night, the fragrance, time spread out over the horizon. Poetry comes out to meet me.

Those distant sands erased the zones of shadow and light. Everything became history after the footsteps, pathways after the dreams. Walking became a dream, the dream turned into a path, and the sand with its impermanence returned us to the perfume of objects.

Always returning to Isla Negra, or perhaps I never left it. The island preserved its stories in dreams that the water tosses and tumbles, or perhaps something of ourselves remained there in that fishermen's cove of hypnotic waters, of sands populated by agate and the voice of Neruda in his home among the pines.

They say it is possible to imagine the texture of the wind over the cliffs at night. With the passing of time, Isla Negra is transformed into a legend, a story that is written and rewritten according to the poems we read on its shores, according to the omens of the inhabitants who choose to remain here, falling in love with the sea and its implacable fury.

Perhaps my desire for the sea had its beginning here among these vast expanses of land, enormous pasturelands, where wild and ferocious horses lived. Of all the places I carried within me during those years of exile, perhaps this was the most beloved. It became a secret pleasure that only I could remember on so many nights, pale nights when loneliness descended over my body like an unflinching knife.

Memory, for those who abandon their beloved places, possesses the undulating power of clarifying what for years soul and mind consider sealed. Isla Negra awoke in me something I perhaps did not know I loved, that feeling of being near the immensity of waves, beside the coast . . . observing the swaying of yellow flowers that covered the earth in wisdom and perfection.

Or letting myself be transported by the caress of a wave wrapped in the mother-of-pearl of desire.

Once my mother told me in her sweet wisdom that the things you love fit in your pockets, like the butterflies my hands caress and save in the coffers of memory, but also like the agates that are collections of light, stones kept in my pockets to accompany voyages.

In that way Isla Negra surrounded me, wrapped itself around my waist, managed to touch my errant happiness, until one day I returned there to confirm that what I had imagined was real, that my soul that wandered about at night was able to feel the astonishment of the world and understand the signs and myths that all the inhabitants strung together as if life were made of water, saltwater that tells stories.

On Isla Negra a group of women embroider life and hope, and as Pablo Neruda says, they all have important names, names that are like flowers, marisol, dahlia, azucena. . . . In winter months when the fishermen leave the sea and dream in hibernation of the arrival of a promising summer, the women take out their enormous woolen tapestries they have kept beneath their beds beside the eucalyptus branches to protect themselves from the spirits of danger.

And their hands descend slowly over the weaving. They embroider life and hope, the passing of days in this cove that is invented according to the omens of the wind. The weavings are daring. They are not afraid of color or the biography that surrounds them. They sketch enormous violet-colored birds, lost fish, hefty hens. And their feet barely leave footprints; they are fleeting angels. They glide pleasantly as in a story, as in a labyrinth where mischievous birds make their nests.

The sand accepts adoration, it is heard in the midst of the ocean's hoarse voice and its foamy attire. Sand recreates the footprints. It erases them, invents them with the breath of the wind, and it refuses to be discovered, because each tracing is like the disorderly pen of the angels that blesses, sings, and explodes, Neruda says. He says everything, absolutely everything, flourishes on the island, but especially the hands of the Marias, the Eduviges, Miss Blanquita who embroiders a beautiful sign saying, "Fresh bread here today." How ironic that he died only days after the 1973 coup that changed the course of our country's history.

I return to Isla Negra in the winters, when the women tell me about their lives, weave stories, and exchange secrets; and from their hands, trees, sighs, and a round table for celebrating the hour of twilight, the fruits of the sea, langostinos and shrimp, and the festivities of the earth burst forth.

The sand conforms to my feet. When I return to my country, I visit it, I bare my feet so it will recognize me and let me submerge my stories over its own. I roll around in it, risk myself completely in it, dream in its purplish yellows, and the sand takes me back to an age before gestures, when touch was pleasure, reminiscence, memory, and happiness.

Outdoors the sand and I, the heart of the sand and the heart of my feet. I return to the coasts of Chile where once my cheek blended with the ear of the wind and I was able to rebuild an imaginary castle on a lost coast whose sand was moved on seeing me appear.

And that is how I feel on the sands of my homeland, fulfilled like a hopeful continent.

Fog

The fog in Isla Negra rushes ever closer to this house made of stone. Sometimes when it is sunny, I rest my cheeks against its walls. I become completely flustered when I feel the coolness of the stones, a tickling sensation covers my entire eleven-year-old body. Could this be what Carmen experiences when she prays? Can this be what Mama says it means to be in love? I like this stone house, the wind on the stones, the sound of the sky opening up and setting free the clouds that settle over the trees.

Nature gazes at me and demands that I return its gaze. Suddenly I see the fog that foretells the approach of the wind and the nostalgia of lost animals. The wind over the southern night lets me hear something like a song on my skin, on my body that is growing too quickly but does not want to cover itself, that dreams of being naked facing the ponds.

The Flower Carvers of Pucón

The flower carvers of Pucón appear at the edge of the roads like angels returning from a dream, surrounded by frost, beyond the cold and its silences. I see them leaning over, with their hands discovering the wood. And from the dark and light wood, the flowers are born, tiny as the origin of the earth, wise and ancient, like secrets hidden by the volcano. In Pucón the women carve flowers out of wood like someone who falls in love with a body and on it carves tattoos of love.

Words

I don't know how or when a love for words was born in me. Was it the sounds, the elongation of the letters, the furrows in a thick piece of paper? I loved the Hebrew letters; they had forms and textures that seemed to be awakening from an ancient dream. My grandmother, before starting her day, when dawn appeared like a golden canvas that barely peeked over the surfaces, would read in Hebrew, silently and aloud. At that moment it was impossible to approach her. She belonged to a distant sovereignty, to a site of prayers that was hers alone; that is what I imagine this memory to be.

Hebrew seemed to me a secret and peaceful language. We lived with it always, but it was the language of prayer, of sacred zones where God and man exchanged the audacity of the secret writings. I also grew up with Yiddish, a mischievous and substantial language, a language capable of cursing and loving with equal fervor, and with the same passion for madness that made us burst into laughter. Mama would tell me sometimes that she needed other people's problems like a hole in the head. Once I heard her say she would like to go far, far away, to the place where black pepper grows, but I do not know where black pepper grows.

Papa—my grandfather—speaks German with Grandmother. Sometimes I think this language is like Yiddish, but it is harsh and has strange intonations. It is rough, like the shouts I hear at times when the girls see me passing by. Nothing about this language appeals to me, but Papa says it is good to know German. I want to learn other languages because it seems to me that they are secret passages to other voices and other things. There is a family here in Santiago from Czechoslovakia. They understand German but they speak Czech.

I like Spanish because languages above all must make us happy, and I play in Spanish. I play blind man's buff and hopscotch, imagining that with a single leap I can conquer the sky or the earth.

I like to write. Papa gave me a notebook without lines. I think I will be a poet. They talk here about a very strange woman named Gabriela Mistral.* They say she has no husband, no children, and they say she does not have a desk, that she writes on her knees while staring at the sky. That is what I want to do, write on my knees that are always trembling.

*Pseudonym of Lucila Godoy Alcayaga, Chilean poet, educator, and diplomat, winner of the 1945 Nobel Prize for Literature.

My Dictionary

Yesterday, Papa presented me with my first Spanish dictionary. It has brown covers, but I see them as mauve, because I like the color purple. I am happy with my dictionary. Each letter tells a story, and this is what Mama and Papa mean when they say that in the beginning of all things words were born, and in the beginning of all words is the heart of the verb, the beginning, the roundness of life. I sit down for hours to gaze at the dictionary that rests on my cello, or the cello on the dictionary, because everything revolves with the words. In the distance, the sound of the countryside and the winter that is never severe but allows us peace and calm. I like to imagine the hills covered with frost, ready for the slowness of sorrows until the next spring.

The earth is calm. I love this place at the bottom of the earth. Mama knows I am happy. Papa takes a stroll. To me, everything seems near and far, big and small, at the same time. I take my notebook out of my pocket and write.

I am happy with my dictionary. I like to receive gifts and give them. Here, everyone gives gifts: fresh bread, butter, garnet bracelets, and half-dried eucalyptus to hide under the beds. I am happy that all this is true, and that letters tell me stories. Someday people will learn how beautiful this country is, and many people will come to visit it. In the meantime, I am happy to be living here. I like to observe everything intensely. If I could, I would be a photographer, but I am a musician, and sounds are like a picture. That is true; nothing can replace the round beauty of the letter *a*.

Words II

My mother says it is useless to struggle with words. I should let them rest easily on objects, on my skirt like butterflies. Grandmother looks out of the corner of her eye. She has the Torah on her lap, and before opening its pages, she kisses it as if it were a very large child dressed as a groom. My father listens to the radio that seems like a distant breeze, a screeching over the night in the countryside where animals announce the sounds of the dead to the living. I listen to the sound of sighing and footsteps on the wooden floors. Even though the war is very far away, it seems like it is close to home. Grandmother prays in Hebrew and in Yiddish.

I am still struggling with the idea of God. What a strange idea of the Jews, who believe that God is one and not triple. All my girlfriends have their favorite virgins, festivals that celebrate virgins dressed in purple and reddish tones. My mother calls them "Las católicas." They make their First Communion and look like angels or snowflakes, and they carry wonderful prints of the Virgin in their pockets. In our house we have only Grandmother's candelabra, sad and dim, and the Torah that Grandmother closes as if life were closing on her too.

It is useless to battle fate, or what others call our origins. My tired body becomes silent. I dream about returning to that wooden bed, rustling in it, imagining the virgin of dew, that mischievous and sinning virgin winking her eye at me.

The Apron of Dreams

Last night I dreamed I was alone in the darkness. The apron that previously was filled with fresh objects was covered in ashes. I felt filled with smoke, with my skin blackened. I told my grandmother about my dream, and she plunged into her customary silences that this time appeared sharper to me, like those knives I would see resting at the end of the kitchen on afternoons when they did not decapitate the chickens or the vegetables.

Carmencha was fond of dreams. She said they had colors and sediments like the textures of the earth. She was always the one who told me of them, and I would write them in my notebook of true and imaginary dreams. The ones that were true were those that occurred to me as I was leaving school, when the girls laughed at me because I did not carry images of angels in my pockets.

Carmencha says it is good to dream about lentils, because they represent abundance, but not when you dream about a dish of lentils at a funeral. In the distance I can hear my grandmother's footsteps. She wants to learn Spanish but refuses. She sketches the rhythm of the journey of birds that mistakenly wander through this house made of wood, stone, and secret things.

The dream comes back to me. I am alone in a forest of fog. I am walking and I carry a menorah on my back, and at my side there is a menorah without branches. Carmencha asks me if my dream has a smell. I tell her yes, it is the smell of death, a smell of where no one and nothing grows. I tell her that in my dream I can only make out dead birds, and in the distance there is no one, nothing.

From that dream I learn that I will understand things from

the margins, from behind, and by what can scarcely be heard. I am afraid of knowing what will come, of dreaming about omens. My grandmother gazes at me, but she already knows about this gift. I return to my room and write nothing, because whatever I write in my diary occurs. I stop in front of the thresholds where the ibises are fluttering around. The fog grows thicker and thicker. I know that winter is approaching when the days are long and the light is scanty. I approach my grandmother, who has not stopped gazing at me. She tells me that every night she dreams of those forests, but there is no fog, no landscape, there are only shadows. On those nights she dreams of her sisters and calls them.

That is how I learn that Grandmother has left so many things behind: sisters, aunts, cousins, rose gardens, and the keys to her house. In her room a padlock hangs without a key. The lock is dark and it grows darker each time I look at it.

Night always comes to Osorno in an unexpected fashion. It is a burst of wind that seethes and glides through the hallways. Night wears the face of the wind. An abysmal silence surrounds us. It is impossible to sleep in so much silence and in such a fearful darkness. Carmencha extinguishes the salamander stove. The last pieces of firewood glow. I fall asleep in front of the embers. I no longer dream.

Naming

Carmen likes to name things, and when she feels lost or excited, she begins to whistle from deep inside her chest, as if she were a misplaced teakettle. When she forgets the names of things, she makes them up, mixing in a little of her Mapuche tongue, and often greeting in German. She loves to sing at times of happiness and dark sadness. Lately she has been cursing in Yiddish and making gestures with her lips that always hold a cigarette she has rolled herself.

I look over old postcards that Grandmother sent. When I approach her to ask about those squares or immense avenues, she smiles but looks into the distance, and her voice is lost. These days, Grandmother stares at the sky, into the void, at the immense borders that cross southern Chile. I see her leaning over the balustrade. She tells me she does not have faith in the stars. Every day Carmen looks at her horoscope in the morning and plays the lottery. My grandmother's faith is strange, as if it were a muddy river or a thing that one should look at cautiously.

Carmen's faith lies in naming objects, in the stars, and in believing that if you stare at yourself too much in the mirror, you will see the dead pass by. I grow up between these two women. I contemplate the stars. I believe in them, in their elegant remoteness, their unconditional passion. Horoscopes make me smile and sometimes blush.

The two of them talk about faith. One says, "Blessed be the Lord," and the other insists that the name of God should not be pronounced. I grow up between silence and the words of silence.

The Victrola

Today Papa brought a giant radio that everyone calls a Victrola. It is a German radio. Everyone here likes things from other places, and no one is at all interested in anything having to do with Chile. Papa has spent the entire afternoon gazing at his Victrola, where he places the records and listens to Viennese operettas. Mama looks at him out of the corner of her eye while she knits her endless scarves that no one likes very much because they lose their shape and become longer and longer. But Papa with his Victrola seems to have returned to Vienna. He puts on his hat to listen to the music and says that well-bred people play piano with their hats on.

Carmencha and I look at him sideways. All this makes me laugh. I too will play the piano, with my blue hat and an ostrich feather I found in an antique shop, the one that sells photos of Hitler with a moustache.

But the Victrola does not excite me as much as the radio in Carmencha's room. The two of us have a permanent appointment at three in the afternoon when I return home from school and begin to listen to the soap operas like a crazy person. Some things are incomprehensible to me, like the idea of a single mother. Mothers are mothers and the idea of being single or married is very confusing. Sometimes it rains on Carmencha's ceiling, and it seems like we are listening to a very strange music caused by flooding. I like it when the doors creak in the soap operas and the wind seems to be a passionate ghost.

Carmen cries over the fate of her favorite characters. She identifies with the poor, and I do too, because they are like the Jews and practically no one likes them. My mother looks at us from the corner of her eye. She is not jealous but Carmen is something else. She smells like maté and herbs. She is tiny, like the first poppies, or very big, like the weeping willow where I hide. I cover myself completely next to her and kiss her. The soap opera comes to an end, the bad guys get what they deserve, and the good guys win. It is always the same, like life and hope.

Teatime

Grandmother prepares the *onces*, the "elevenses." That is what we call teatime in Chile. It comes from the English, the maids always say, in the back rooms. It comes from the word *eleven*, says Grandmother, in an English that sounds more like a Yiddish accent than a British one. I like to listen to Grandmother preparing the table. She takes out the tablecloth from Venice, the wineglasses from Vienna, the English marmalades. Only the bread is from Chile, but they call it a croissant, the way they do in Argentina.

I feel that the world exists in other places. Grandmother sings in Yiddish and says she is off-key because she is hungry. Delfina curses in Mapundungun; she sings her mother tongue that is secret, and perhaps she will share it with me. I like this teatime. Grandmother takes out the fine china. She also eats the bread with melted cheese with her teeth firmly fixed; that is, she decides not to remove them. And they talk of so many things, each woman on her own topic—shared monologues, says the one who considers herself most intelligent, most wise. But they are together, they observe the occasion, they look at one another, see one another, always come close to one another, and when saying goodbye accompanied by the perfume of strawberries and whipped cream, they promise to see one another the following week to joyously repeat this tea ceremony, this delightful reunion. Grandmother grumbles because there are too many crumbs on the tablecloth and her napkins are stained with avocado. She decides to remove her teeth and smiles. I look at her and say, "This is happiness," what happens after tea.

Inside My House

I stand in front of the cut glass picture windows, faced with what others might call sadness, but for me it is the texture of the soul. I wait for the rain hopefully, as I do all the days of the year. I already recognize the sound of the *bandurrias*, the ibises that cross the cordillera of the Andes toward Argentina. Sometimes I am absolutely convinced that this is the best life we have been destined to live: removed from hate, anchored to the slowness of the rhythm of snack time, teatime, the setting of the sun.

Here at the end of the world, I learn the lessons of the rain. It comes slowly, like a subtle whisper, or like one of those guests who decide not to stay very long. The rain is a transitory guest that, after being carried away, wishes to remain astonished about things and not desist in its tenacity. It rains on this house throughout a long, extended winter. All the same, we learn to love this rain that shows us the slowness of the hours, the possibility of understanding ourselves through a sound that is the repetition and imagination of things at a distance.

Every afternoon I rest my heart and my ear on the rain. I recognize and imagine myself. I hear the footsteps of the house, the sweeping brooms. I imagine my grandmother's memory that is perhaps the memory of a wall or an abyss, and slowly I invent for myself stories in the distance.

The true guest in the house is the rain, with its foggy curtains, its ribbons the color of ashes. Grandmother dreams about northern things, here in the south with its snowy forests and lost cousins. I embrace her from behind, to play with her ashen hair, and tell her to dare to understand silent things through the rain and its closed spaces, its silences and its constancy like love.

Little Souls

At the edge of the roads where the horizon blends with sand, and the sea with ashes, there beyond time and history, shrines, little souls* pointing out the pathways. The little souls and their great accomplishments in life and their miracles in death. I always thought about them, especially on the roads in the south of Chile, foggy, winding roads where suddenly the way becomes lost. The roads became bridges of stagnant waters, and there was no way to go on, no way to return, and we remained suspended, hoping that something would happen, like the story of the miracles. And suddenly, the little souls like colored angels, hinting at the possibility of another path, another road to follow.

Often there were small inscriptions on the cross inside the little soul, because it was like a house, a little house of colors that reminded me of the color of the angels, the color of the sky. The little souls suffered violent deaths, suicides, gunshots, premature accidents. They were there as reminders of lives cut short, but I also saw in them the possibility of understanding present lives, of understanding this life through the omen that death shows us.

Did Jews have little souls? What were the routes of the soul, its pathways? I used to ask, Where is the Holy Spirit? Who is, what is the Trinity? I wanted to believe in things. Sometimes the God of the Jews was invisible. My father would recite the Shema Israel, which means, "Hear, O Israel." But who would hear me? Who would recognize us in this loneliness? Then I would go wild

---

*Animitas, or little souls, are small shrines at the side of the road marking the site of an unusually violent death. People come to pray and ask favors of these often miraculous spirits.

over the little souls in their little white houses, becoming part of the density of life, the roots of the earth. I sought the answer in them. A voice. The possibility of love and faith. But faith lay in believing, in knowing that in the bifurcation of these paths, we would find something. A story, a rose watching over a heart grown dark. Faith lay in accepting the unknown, the enigmas promised by the pathways.

Words III

At night I yearned to be transported by words, the tender ones I heard at home, braided with Yiddish and Spanish, or the words that could not be heard, those that were understandable only through silence. Those words at home were guarded by fear. That is how I grew up, between the clanking of objects and the unspeakable. When words became scarce, Grandmother would take out her prayer book, and her hands became leaves, and her pen danced over the letters. Slowly I dared to enter deeply into them, to feel the peace of their curves as they touched my palate among the stories. They taught me to be generous, to learn to use them with moderation, and not to let them decay because of human mendacity.

On those long nights I would remove my notebook of dreams from a rusty chest. My father, who was on the other side of the room, on the other side of the world, would remove his travel journal and list his unsuccessful love affairs and unspoken words and at the same time send out indecipherable messages. I began to record life, with its trifles and its grandeur, with the peace of promises made in childhood and fulfilled on the thresholds of death. Salvation lies in invisible spaces, in the syllables braided on my fingers. And so I wrote and I write.

Languages of Home

The languages in our home flowed like currents of air, some like diaphanous spirits, and others that were too heavy. Yiddish was used for cursing or for laughing at ourselves. Spanish made us feel like rulers over our days, our landscape, and our lives. For me, Ladino was one of the languages that occupied the seat of honor between mystery and ambiguity, between the sadness that is carried deep in one's soul and the joy that erupts from song.

Miss Victoria, who used to visit us often, bringing crescent-shaped cookies, would say that she wanted to return to Sepharad, to Spain, the true promised land, and so she would start to sing, like a well of fresh water, the old songs heard, sung, and preserved by other women. Songs are meant for treasuring, honoring, and sharing. One day she began to tell me stories about Christopher Columbus, Queen Isabella, Juan de Torres, and this America that opened its doors for those Jewish converts to live in secret but, at the same time, to practice the rhythm of their faith.

My Cello

I still do not know how my father acquired the cello that travels with me as if we were a single house turned upside down by the sound of things. In the south of Chile, the cello resembled the sound certain birds make at the hour of awakening; it became part of the landscape; it joined the migration of the herons. These sounds of early childhood were of forests recording the tempestuous sound of the rain or the era of peaceful things, when the clarity of the forest is a bell and birds return to our old wooden house.

Slowly we grew older, we discovered Elgar and Bach, we drowned in sounds and sobbing. I grew to understand that the purpose of music was to achieve goodness and peace. The day before we left Chile, I took my cello to the old Jewish cemetery in Conchalí. The dead were asleep, but I left signs on the graves, kissing the Star of David and playing Bruch's *Kol Nidrei*. It was a cloudy day, but the heavens opened up and there was peace in the sky. The following morning I left. From high above I gazed at this landscape and imagined I was recapturing it through the sound of loving words I repeated to myself. I felt that my soul was hollow, that I was part of a people and a history of ghosts, and I remembered my house made of wood, the silence and the sound of green leaves. I saw myself among the ferns, barefoot in the streams or in the house of Frida Haase as she bowed before the dead.

Music managed to find the best part of me. More than words, it was that buried melody that managed to convey my feelings. Through my cello I grew to understand farewell gestures, the sinuosity of night and the cavities of silence. At night my cello and I shared more than sound, because the instrument became memory and a fragment of melodies, the whistle of a lost train or the cry of my grandparents when they begged for life. The cello greeted the footsteps of the dead and the beginning of the time of the living.

The cello and I remembered those simple days when the world seemed like a postcard. I remember my father at the train station. He, the cello, and I welcomed refugees with eyes of wanderers, eyes with sunken sockets.

I understood that all of time is an easily frightened chord that seems to play by itself in the immensity of the air.

As in paintings by Chagall, I saw everything from the sky; I saw peaceful things, kisses between lovers during the dark siestas of the south, the trilling of birds when guests arrive, and my grandmother with her silver candelabra and her faith that is like a pack filled with provisions that maintain me, and which I carry with me now.

My Father

My father is small and says only what is necessary; I have become used to his silences that suddenly take solid form as words. He loves poetry and biochemistry, and at night when he thinks we are all asleep, he plays Chopin.

My father studied medicine during difficult times, when Nazism in Chile had a face and boots. He often recounts how during the time of the Second World War he was persecuted so many times and people would say, "There goes the Jew," but he pursued his career in medicine. He played the piano until midnight in my grandmother's house, where he rented a room. That is how he met my mother. She says she fell in love with him when she heard him playing Chopin's nocturnes in the wee hours of the night.

When he graduated as a doctor, he refused to practice, because he did not have the heart to charge the poor. He practiced for only a month, and my mother stayed in the office with him all the time, as if she were a patient. She was the healthiest and most beautiful patient in an office empty except for the occasional penniless person, who paid for his services with a dozen eggs, but my father preferred to investigate hidden things, what the microscope hides and reveals.

Violeta Parra

Yesterday Violeta Parra* committed suicide in her tent in La Reina, where heaven and earth are hidden and the rain never ceased. All the newspapers talk about her life, and I think perhaps they are telling the truth, that she killed herself for love. I respect not only her suicide, but her life also. It is the winter of 1967; I am an impressionable adolescent. The wooden houses of my country sob, and the rafters of the high roofs seem to thrash about from grief. I remember the days in Osorno that seemed like night, when the rain was our only guest and the wind seemed to moan like a lost bird.

Now in Santiago, this winter marks the suicide of Violeta. She was childhood and innocence, a challenging presence. Her voice belonged to this world and the other. The divine and the human were intertwined in a sound of gratitude in time with time. While all the radios of the country announce her death, and on the hill where she lived torches appear, I gaze at the rain and the sky with my eyes open, and I make certain that Violeta Parra has died and that she has not gone to the promised land, since her paradise was this land. Today I hear her echoes and her footsteps, and only her soul illuminates this night that is as long and solitary as this land.

---

*The well-known singer and composer of countless Chilean folk songs—the most famous of them "Gracias a la vida" (Thanks to life)—and sister of the poet Nicanor Parra.

Words IV

I began to feel them fluttering slowly, fleetingly, cheerfully, flirtatiously. I sensed them as if they were puffs of air—so delightful to feel them, to see them pass by, to see them smile while mischievously they tried to emerge, to touch the world, to slip within your ear, to make you laugh.

I loved them from childhood and could not restrain them. They burst forth, bewitched me, made me fall in love. I caressed them at night, or in what seemed to me to be the night. They resembled sorceresses, fleeting stars, golden dust. They beckoned me and I followed them like a child in love with the circus or a comet.

In order not to forget them, I jotted them down in enormous notebooks, silky and disorderly opaline notebooks, notebooks with the rhythm of topaz, and carried them inside me as if they were a night within night, a prayer within a dream.

And suddenly, history abandoned me. I was cold crossing the cordillera. Who would I be within these stories? Who would I love with them? Shipwrecked without my language, and everything around smelled of ice fields, of nostalgia filled with certainty, of things that flee in the night.

But the words did not abandon me. I illuminated alphabets with them, sought certainty, called the dead, and so they returned to my side again, to kneel at those moments when the fire of neglect consumed and abandoned me.

Growing older with them. The story that grieved me so much

helped me to grow. Words that accompany me when I go to the market or repeat names aloud, lethargic words, words I pronounce as I kiss you, and your mouth, our mouths, fill up with garlands, words that crown truth and history, that judge the guilty, that play with the melody of language.

Night

Night has fallen even faster over the Osorno sky. It is strange, this night at the beginning of the month of March, when the winds are warm; and the rhythms of time, clear. We have decided to leave this mean little village with its German club, the German school, and the German women who sometimes whisper when they see us passing by. My grandmother has wrapped up as always her few belongings. From the house she saves only the candelabra, the padlock from the front door, and the glances of rejection from her neighbors who had chatted for years about the lilies, the flowers, and the imperial avenues. When the order of arrest and confiscation of properties arrived, my grandmother says, no one knocked at the door to wish her a peaceful odyssey. Without looking back, she embarked toward the end of the earth, the most southern reaches of the planet.

Today, we too are leaving. These arrivals and departures are part of our education, like being born with a suitcase always in our hands. My mother is taking a blue envelope with her first love letters. I am standing in front of the train station with my cello and a parrot my father recently gave me.

In the distance my schoolmates arrive, a very poor band that used to play Viennese waltzes and music by Brahms every Sunday in the plaza. Papa wipes his eyes. Mama gazes into the distance. The train seems like a toy: it is red and the locomotive seems like a song from the Alps. The capital is progress, longing, and beauty, Mama says, and so we set off for a better life. Behind us lies the empty house, unmade beds, an empty fireplace, and we are no longer the same.

⊰ Part II ⊱
The Times of Darkness

Prelude II

Santiago 1970, a Joyful Morning

At first I felt an unexpected joy, a throbbing that was disturbing yet comforting. Salvador Allende* was elected by a very small margin of votes. Chilean law upheld his triumph. That night we went out on the street. My parents were still living in a dilapidated house downtown, the same house where we used to dream about another life from the balconies shaken by the wind that foretold collapses as well as the numerous earthquakes or tremors of the soul that threatened the city.

This time I imagined that the balcony also felt jubilant, filled with hope and possibilities that one dares only to dream about. This time I really did dream of a different life, and it was true. Just as my parents had told me how, at the end of the Second World War, the avenues were filled with rose petals, and the women who sold flowers transformed the streets of Santiago into a concert of leaves, today I felt that same luminescence, that beauty that is born from things within us.

We all went out to the streets carrying drums and flags. More than a political triumph, this is an election filled with innocence, and we feel happy as we recognize one another. We look at one another and say, "Hello, comrade." That word implies peace, solidarity, and the possibility of a new life.

They say that in the wealthy neighborhoods they bolted their doors with enormous locks of fear and hid the jewelry and cham-

---

*1908–1973, Socialist Party candidate and Marxist politician, elected president of Chile in 1970; died during the Pinochet coup on September 11, 1973.

pagne. I saw none of this, but perhaps it was true. Fear took control of their meaningless lives. In the poor neighborhoods, people lit bonfires. It was the month of September, and you could still smell the aroma of fresh chestnuts, light, and new stories in the air.

I go to Italy Square carrying the cello I always kept with me, because as a Jew, I grew up with the possibility of fleeing. I played among the crowds that were approaching with curiosity, but then they stopped beside us in respectful silence. I played "The International," and for the first time I did not feel like the daughter of refugees, nor was I aware of being a woman. I was only a note suspended in a golden horizon, a noble note that emerged from the very heart of my cello.

The Night before the Coup

It was a glorious day; spring was approaching wrathfully, like life that was experienced fully. Never did I feel more carefree or more in love with rhythms, the possibility of just being and creating objects, stories, and poems.

The night before the coup I said good night to my nocturnal poppy, just as I did every night. I sensed its sadness. I recognized the bent shape of its figure and its distant gaze. I wanted to learn things from it and remember its birth. The day it arrived on the balcony, it was all light and reddish at the same time. I kept its image in my hands when I planted it like a lost angel.

That night I dreamed about my grandmother when she learned her first words in Spanish. Her handwriting was an enormous spider in love with the crevices and secret spaces, with a voice that speaks and does not speak at the same time.

In solitude I created that little night. I tried to see the world in miniature. I felt an inexplicable fear, but at the same time a certainty that day would return. It was the month of September, and the forsythia was blooming, ablaze with love and shades of yellow.

Ordinary Women

In the Santiago mornings I generally awaken in a state of happiness. I have always been grateful knowing I was alive, blessing all things, living and dead. Our house always seems to be gazing toward the mountain range, as if the entire country were a single privileged horizon. But that morning I woke up differently.

Around me I sensed the musty odor of dying weeds and sleeping honeysuckle. I went out to the street. Spring was late in announcing itself and did not seem to appear with the tenacity of other years. The wild yellow forsythia covering the window remained opaque.

Ordinary women went out early as they always did in search of bread and words. Clementina, who had this wondrous obsession with cleaning the sidewalks at dawn and covering them with fresh roses, was left dumbfounded, like Lot's wife. In the distance, wild birds with faces of owls and emblems of war began to flutter over the city. Suddenly I realized why I had awakened differently.

That morning, September 11, 1973, children went to school, little girls dirtied their white aprons, and suddenly the sky was dressed in black, the day became a perpetual mourning. Airplanes gone mad unfurled their arrogant march and exploded bombs over La Moneda. A wreath of smoke covered the presidential palace.

We awakened transformed. It was that sense of betrayal and fear the air brought back to us, of future days when we would become strangers, and our neighbors informants. I woke up strangely, as if I had dry grass in my mouth. The scene changed.

This silence was a terrifying blow. The only things we heard were the sounds of the radio playing national anthems. There was no voice, no hissing. The sky remained clear and astonished. I felt like a different person, and this is why I was afraid. I drank my coffee and could not greet my country.

Language became ever more diminished, and a decorous silence appeared and covered us and disclosed us. The fluttering birds were airplanes with faces of frightened men.

I returned home, where solitude seemed to be a whisper within the empty walls. The neighbors had vanished in a haze of smoke, and I was left alone with my cello leaning next to the balustrade. Far away, where the horizon is a fringe split in two, black birds flutter over the city. I think about my grandmother Helena when she left Vienna on that summer night when the beautiful weather contradicted the stories of horror, when night seemed to be a stole made of garnets.

This spring appears slowly but wrathfully. The color yellow fills the view. I feel a tremendous silence invading me that grieves me and lulls me to sleep.

The Death of Salvador Allende

Yesterday the army murdered President Salvador Allende, although they say he committed suicide. That morning a wrathful spring appeared to test the first buds of the dawn. I have always been accustomed to living life elegantly, awakening at later hours, drinking my coffee with milk at a leisurely pace. I opened the shutters and felt as if the previous night had drowned me in a turbulent river.

At eleven in the morning yesterday, we felt the bombings, and the sky seemed to collapse upon us. We turned on the radio and heard the horrifying military marches. Helicopters plowed through Santiago's sky. Smoke seemed to overpower us, and a frightful nightmare enveloped us.

I closed the windows. I sat down and realized we would be leaving soon. I refused to allow memory to become weak or seem like a ghostly outline that moves away and is slowly resuscitated over the immensity of history. I insisted upon memory becoming an obsession, the certain presence of those nights of insomnia, those somnambulant seasons.

I refused to let go of my mother's face, gazing stubbornly in the direction of the flames, or my grandmother's, arranging photographs, composing stories and taking them apart again, invisible fabrics of truncated lives. I wanted all of this to become clarity and memory, a symphony of strings resting in my hands. I learned to repeat my grandmothers' stories, the color of fruit, the sense of taste. I want to conclude my story and not unmask its face or the faces of those who are gone. I want everything to be history, color, the dream of each and every night.

They say Salvador Allende was too naive, that he trusted General Pinochet too much. Allende said he was a man of great confidence and cunning. But history revealed something different: General Pinochet was not a man worthy of trust. On the contrary, this general sowed the seeds of hatred. He was the instigator of terrorism, and later of fear.

The Disappeared

People are beginning to disappear. We dare not name them. They disappear at night or in broad daylight. I am afraid to look at the muddy and heart-rending rivers, rivers that carry bones. They say that at night soldiers pound on the doors, knock them down, and take them away, never to return, or perhaps to return and talk about the fear, feel the fear and pain within their brittle skin.

I am afraid of the void, the faces of those I love who now are becoming more and more opaque, and it seems we are letting ourselves be carried away by doubt, by the exercises of death, by grief.

Some go to the National Stadium. They are detained for hours or days. People form tremendous lines outside, and the women shout, begging for mercy. Now I know what it means to live without all hope, the uncertainty, that oppression. Our faces are different now; young girls have become old women. They wear skirts, jeans are forbidden. I refuse to live like that. Tomorrow I may be the one who is searching, the one who disappears. The line is tenuous. Someone shouts that we are still alive.

I return home. I no longer gaze at the stars. The sky over Chile is clouded and seems to be a strange cemetery. I want to leave, but no flight seems possible to me. I am afraid, but it is a fear of the arbitrary nature of things.

Victor Jara

Rumor says they have murdered Victor Jara* in the National Stadium, where there are thousands of detainees. Before, it was a place to play soccer and have picnics with our families. Today, they say the soldiers cut off his fingers and then his hands, but he kept on singing and thanked all those who still loved what his song conveyed—happiness and solidarity. Victor sang like a nightingale in love, but more than anything, like a man committed to history and the people.

At night I hear the sounds of maimed guitars, the moaning of widows and orphans. Victor Jara has died but still sings.

---

* 1932–1973, Chilean poet, singer, songwriter, and human rights activist, who was tortured and murdered after the Pinochet coup.

Charles Horman

They are investigating the death of the American student Charles Horman,* but we all know the State Department knew about his death five days after the coup. Charles's father and his widow filed a suit against the North American authorities. We know the CIA arrived months earlier to plan the coup. My grandmother said you could see American Marines strolling through the port looking for girls and teaching young Chilean soldiers the mechanics of murder.

They say Charles knew too much, that his camera was able to record everything, to remember everything. They say the State Department planned his murder and that they knew exactly when he was shot.

We live days of fear and deception; we forget the real questions, because everything, absolutely everything, exists in a void.

Now we know they have murdered Charles Horman and Frank Teruggi. The press only repeats over and over that they are two Americans, as if their nationality were more important than their deaths. I met Charles in one of those cafés in the Bellavista district. He loved music and Chile. He was also obsessed with sketching everything he saw. He was barely twenty years old. No one knows where they died or where they took them. This is a land of questions where no one gives answers, where no one says more than what is absolutely necessary for survival. The neighbors say that at five thirty an armored car came in search of Charles, and that was the last they knew. We all search in silence.

*The movie *Missing* was based on the disappearance of Horman in Chile during the coup.

"Tonight I Can Write the Saddest Verses"*
The Funeral of Pablo Neruda, September 1973

Yesterday they held a wake for Pablo Neruda in his home in Santiago. The military guarded the house they had sacked days earlier. Matilde is calm. That is what they say, and she remains firm in the face of the military's orders to not allow anyone to enter. Little by little, the house fills with poets, musicians, and fortune-tellers. The poet's home opens slowly. It is spring and night falls in love with its own perfume. People arrive all night long to pay tribute to that wonderful sleeping body, filled with words, ideas, and games. Neruda's voice is not only in his books, but also in all of us. The house of poetry remains open. He drank tea at dawn, and I felt he had left us much too soon. Someone recited one of his poems, and the house was filled with the sound of bells and light melodies. I knew at that moment that poetry had not died, and that Neruda is alive, now and forever, our comrade is present.

Yesterday they buried Pablo Neruda. Memories are vague. Memory seems to be a lethargy of mists that extends ever closer to my face. His verses are now only whispers of fleeting things. My mother took me to the flower market where the women flower vendors of my beloved country would gather, on what now seems to me a very dark night. All of Santiago is covered with flowers. In the distance I feel that history is repeating itself. My country's freedom has come to an end, and the most sonorous and marvelous voice of this continent has died. It was the voice that taught us the meaning of objects, the rhythm of bells, the melodies of things hidden by the sea.

We began to walk and to recognize one another, to feel the

*The first line of one of Neruda's love poems.

passion and throbbing of living things. I felt peace glide along the windowpanes of the poet's house, where he used to wave to us with pencils in the form of kites. I recognized friends from the university and my high school. For the first time, I think I felt that we Jews were definitely a part of the history of this country. I was finally Chilean, what I always wanted to be. They sang "The International" and said that our comrade Neruda was not dead, and word spread across the mountain ranges, and I could recognize the faces of those who had fled, among them my grandparents, who journeyed from cities that no longer exist, where they burned Jews in festive bonfires. I moved away among the weeds. I was hypnotized by the singing and the weather. Nothing within me perished. Each cell lived within me. I was filled with amazement, and I felt that the shanty dwellers had also come, and the women were wearing white scarves and singing and dancing. I felt all of this, and I write it today in this diary I call again my notebook of dreams.

I have always wondered if the soldiers were ashamed of that looting, that discord. They too remain with their heads bowed in front of the thresholds. I often felt pity for them. They must have been innocent young men, their faces now painted black and hatred in their eyes.

How different has this history of Chile been from other histories? What happened between 1946 and 1952, during the era of leftist president González Videla? My father said that at night, in silence, they shot many in the midst of the worst rancor, that which originates between people who know each other, and who perhaps, one day, loved each other.

Musings on Don Pablo

I still remember and sometimes stop remembering when they buried Pablo Neruda. Many people accompanied him, and the march was solemn. I imagined on that rainy and menacing day in the month of September that even the sea missed him, that it had turned ashen and had withdrawn into itself like the color of the sky before the prophecy of storms.

Slowly some people approached. They did not make noise. They seemed to be barefoot, but at every moment there were more of us, like an undeniable surge, like a piece of memory that joined other pieces of memory. We were a victorious memory, and someone within the crowds sang with a clear voice, the voice of a sonorous bell, a voice of peace and hope in the middle of the debris, in a country still in flames.

I had gone out with my cello. I tried to sit down on a straw chair that an old woman carried next to her, while she stopped within a tumult that grew ever more intense, but neither I nor my cello spoke. We did not have words or stories, only the voice of the air and the music that was like a gag. Then I understood that my cello demanded silence of me, that it preferred to remain hidden among the uncertainty, that it wanted neither glory nor prayers, only a silence close to the twilight that was nearing. Someone washed away our sadness with rose petals, and the music came from the air, the earth, the skies. Someone cried, "Viva Allende! Viva Neruda!" and the chorus was like a cello that grew beyond the sky and the clouds that covered us all with a protecting deluge on that long afternoon. It was not the end of a life, but the beginning of our own, in memory, in the refusal to forget.

Patio 29

Unnamed Graves

It is difficult to imagine the streets today, that void that over-whelms and obstructs movements. Before, life seemed to emerge from the present, from the roots of things and time.

Yesterday I ventured into the main cemetery of Santiago, to Patio 29, where they say every night remains of the disappeared are deposited, and at daybreak, mothers search desperately for a fragment of a hand, a foot, or a life that belongs to everyone, but especially to them. The mothers surround the cemetery as if it were a country that belonged to them and arrive there determined to find a bone, a hand, or a history and make it their own.

Human life is distorted. Feelings and eyes are hidden. The mothers sit down, close to the ground. There are no trees or shade, only a gnawing memory sometimes, a memory like a suspended and open wound. The mothers lean over the earth. Night and day create an enormous sobbing, and someone draws names on the damp grass. Beyond time and night, the moon points out another body that arrives, and in the midst of the fog, a mother leans over to kiss it beside the moist earth. In spite of everything, I know she loves this land that gave them both life and death.

At night the moon watches over the trajectory of the dead, and I, on a very fragile balcony, can only remember. I gaze at everything from near and far. I return home and wonder who will remember the anonymous dead of my country. I remember my father used to visit the graves in the remote cemetery of the poor in Valparaíso, and that is what I do, without even realizing it.

Women in the Frost

Terror lay in our becoming accustomed to everything: the silence, long nights graceless as a languid curfew, bitter mornings. Always silence, an enormous silence covering us, besieging us. It was a withered, downcast silence. Besides, there were the disappeared, absent at every moment, those we were always waiting for and who did not arrive at dinnertime or nighttime, at the time for loving. I recall my friend Irma Muller, whose son Jorge disappeared, and my mother's friends, all women, mothers, seekers. Sometimes I felt that all the women swayed at midnight, they went out in the frost and the darkness to search for them.

For years it was always the same: the mothers of the disappeared pounding on doors that no one opened, out of fear, indifference, or the terror that existed everywhere. You could see only the disrespect of those who claimed to know nothing about the matter. The women, always the women, waiting with poppies in their lifeless hair.

November 1, The Day of the Dead

Suddenly a deep silence overcomes me, a silence that lasts one night, or perhaps it is a night that lasts for years. The country and I have become dark. Fear dominates us; from the earliest hours of the morning we become obedient creatures. At night we return home, carrying out the functions that assure our ephemeral survival. At night I go out on the balcony of my city that is now only the city of my dead grandparents. I recognize the stars but my face does not accept any gaze. The roses are drying up, the hyacinths do not bloom, and the forsythia does not display the same shade of yellow. Around me, the air itself is strange.

Since childhood I have loved to play with flour, letting it slip through my hands, realizing that later it will become bread, sustenance of our days. Sometimes I liked to make mountains out of it, beat an egg and pretend it was a sublime volcano. I did not learn any wonderful recipes, but I did learn to feel humility and passion for bread, for the braided crown that covered the table. My grandmother would make challah on Fridays and Sundays; the women of the town seemed like queens selling their kneaded bread. In the smell of these beloved things, I found happiness.

Those memories become more remote when I hear they are arresting people, carrying them off in the middle of the night. Sometimes my friends tell me they sleep with their clothes on, ready to be taken away. Still, I continue to wear silk at night. I tell myself the stories of a thousand and one nights that I heard beside a brazier at the end of the world.

The First Poppies of Summer

Yesterday I dreamed I was a child but spoke the words of an adult. I imagined myself an explorer, crossing forests and thirsting for love as I discovered the first poppies of summer. I also dreamed of this city with a gigantic and feverish wall. I wanted to cross the mountain range and find the ocean. I woke up forever transformed, as I have been since this month of September that seems ever more menacing and wrathful to me. Today I walked through the university campus surrounded by whitewashed walls, covered before with murals, but now with an empty life and an invisible, erased history.

The Students

The students erect low barricades with sacks of flour and American products. The universities are closed, but students sing "The International," loving one another in the open spaces of their classrooms. Everything about them, and me, is air, transparency, and the beauty of living things. The soldiers cover their faces with night and hate. Night is sharp, sinister, and out of tune. They remain there every night, watching over the fragility of that school that may explode momentarily and lose its history. The women brush each other's hair. They sleep in their clothes. They say they do not believe in God, but they pray. And so another night passes at the bottom of the world, where hope still rustles among the rubble.

The Silence of the Humiliated

About the torture, I maintain only the silence of the humiliated. I discovered it as I caressed Antonio Skármeta, the writer, who wrote the book that became *Il Postino*, the story of Pablo Neruda on the Isle of Capri, and his back spoke to me of the signs of the well unfolded by his absence. Suddenly he told me about the unmentionable, what occurs and is remembered only by one who was there. The torture took place in the port of Valparaíso, in the hold of a beautiful sailing ship named *La Esmeralda*.

When he was nothing but sound and a puff of air, he told me he remembered my mother and me constantly gazing in the direction of the port, and for him, our faces were a source of light.

Calendars of Uncertain Times

The calendar lies suspended in indefinite time. We think only about the moment, but this moment is tinged with the survival of our lives. The soldiers have turned into heroes, but only months before, they were labeled filthy Indians. I feel myself constantly gazing toward the Andes Mountains. We have always felt like islanders, cut off from the rest of the world, receiving strangers with hospitality and curiosity. Now the mountains offer us escape routes. Friends of mine have crossed the mountains dressed as nuns or Gypsies. Someday I too will have to leave this country the way my grandmother Helena left Vienna in 1938, in the early fires of the Holocaust. Meanwhile, the hours pass by each other and are interwoven, conversing among themselves. I am surprised by my own passivity that one day may be transformed into a fearful indifference.

Torture

Torture has become an everyday event. We become accustomed to its sounds and movements. All night long a woman screams. She does not name names. She is no longer afraid, because she has lost her fear and her name, but they demand more names. They demand stories, addresses, notebooks. The woman takes refuge in a body of silence and indifference.

The newspapers say it is not true that women have been raped and that people have disappeared. The U.S. State Department says Pinochet is a responsible person and that we must be patient.

Little by little you can hear the chatter, the silence that still seems like a gag or a menacing cloud that rises without haste. Fear still exists, an inexplicable and undefined fear. Neighbors are now strangers, even informants, and strangers have become friends. Night is long, profound and hushed; it is a well of doubts.

They say people keep disappearing. In the middle of the night you hear pounding on the door. Men with painted faces appear and carry them off, no one knows where. The country whispers, "Where are they? Where are they?" It is the only question that is heard, but no one knows the answer. Where are they taken, and why? Some are young men; others, pregnant women and teachers. No one returns, and those who do are no longer the same; they have fear in their faces, a distorted glance.

I too ask, Where are they?

Laughter in the Palace of Madness

They say there is a certain laughter in the palace of madness, and on summer nights at the southern tip of the world, at the south of the imagination, this laughter is heard, but it is not laughter, it is not moaning, it is howling. At night in the city of Santiago, death and torture are accomplices. You can hear the music from the discos in perverse places like Villa Grimaldi or Sexy Blindfold, where all night long the DINA, Pinochet's secret intelligence service, performs its torture. No one ever returns whole from those places where they have been tortured; perhaps the only ones to come back are those forced to be informers who stop on the corners and arrest the suspicious, those with long hair and those who carry poems by Neruda under their arms.

Everything within us turns into absence. We keep losing our words and the places where we tattooed history. Our voices are thin, like the melody of a sailboat lost in the distance. Everything is at a distance and savage within our solitude.

At night we sleep with the windows closed in a world that is closed forever. Here everyone is a torturer, from the soldiers to the police, but silence covers the walls, the ivy dries up. We die slowly.

Traveling Light

Grandmother used to say it was better to travel light and always be ready to flee. Her words become lighter at this troubled time, as I pack my belongings while the house sleeps and the loneliness of not having a homeland appears to me like a shattered mirror.

I no longer know the rhythm of my face and my history. I try to remember the migrations of others. The day when Grandmother left Vienna with her suit the color of garnets and, on the low neckline of her holiday outfit, a blue dragon. She headed south, traveling light.

Again I pack and unpack. What shall I take to America? I store my memories in a suitcase. Shall I take the first crystal lamp, like a Tiffany, that my parents made for me in the squalid back room of a shop, or the photos that were saved from before the war?

I am not afraid of leaving but of returning. Now they are murdering young people simply for being young and for believing. The cello is under my bed, and I hide next to it until dawn.

Red Carnations

Yesterday the mothers of the disappeared bound themselves to the iron grille of the National Congress. They seemed like displaced birds to me, lost essences plundering the traces of night and day as they try to find their way home. Small and dark, they seemed to be a single body, a single chorus of voices, a single story in the proximity of the morning. They chained themselves to the gates of the National Congress, the symbol of Chile, of order and peace in a country of orders camouflaged as a false peace that conceals silence, torture, and the proper obedience.

The women stretch out ever closer to the gates of Congress, and I watch them grow. They seem like fairies, stories of a sparkling night, butterflies. They do not speak, they only gaze at us, and in that gaze is the world of their disappeared children, their lost caresses. In that gaze are all of us and none of us.

The passersby stop. It is impossible to ignore them. It would be impossible to say goodbye to them or to leave them alone in the outdoors, in the mortal remains of history and fear.

They have been on a hunger strike for more than two days, but they are not hungry, thirsty, or cold; they simply gaze beyond the emptiness and present the police with red carnations, nothing more. In those carnations we see life, the world becoming extraordinary and beautiful.

And in this desolate land there are still heroic gestures: a red carnation among the padlocks of the iron grilles of Congress.

The Burning of Books

My political consciousness began in the sixties, when the country was in the midst of great political changes, such as land reform. This took place during the administration of Eduardo Frei. Later, social reforms increased with the advent of Salvador Allende's socialist government in 1970. Unfortunately, this administration lasted only a thousand days, and Pinochet's dictatorship plunged us into dark and terrifying days. When they began to burn books, I realized they wished to burn our ideas, our poetry, our dreams. They wanted to eliminate minds that privileged the truth. And so I realized that Chile was no longer that country that dreamed of justice and food for all. I felt that the world as we knew it no longer existed and we were living among shadows.

History repeats itself and dances with similar movements. My blue suitcase waits. In it I carry my great-grandmother's photo, in my hands the garnet bracelet, and in my memory, the Sabbath prayers, the lullabies she used to sing to me, and that guardian angel she gave me when she arrived in this land she loved so much, even though she was always a stranger here. She also saw the burning of books, in Berlin and again in Chile.

Tomorrow I will leave Chile, a land that previously gave us refuge, but which now has been transformed into a sinister prison where we live mute and masked, surrounded by unspoken words.

I will sleep in another country and learn another language as my ancestors did. I will be faithful to my accent and follow the advice of my grandmother. I will think about my words and draw close only to those that embrace, those that do not threaten. I promise you I will have my discussions with God from time to time.

Embroidering Hope

The Chilean *Arpilleras*

The women embroider hope, the illuminated love of days; they embroider death and the overbearing need to rescue life. The women of my country embroider in the deepest darkness when the gendarmes doze, while the disappeared, the invisible ones, the ones in damp cellars, imagine a butterfly behind the balustrades. And these mothers embroider beds, chairs, clothing of the living and the dead. In my country the women embroidered the history of those who disappeared one day from the high schools, the backyards, the primary schools, and from the plentitude of so, so much life. The women embroider, and their hands are transformed into pathways, histories. Scraps of usurped life now united by the heartbreaking pain, by the hope of retelling.

Gradually, "disappeared" becomes an everyday word, and we become accustomed to saying, "They disappeared." Everything we had invented, even a new vocabulary to express love, remains behind in the rubble, in the threats of fear, and we too disappear, observers of the pit of our own silences.

Calama

And the sun is flaming hot from early morn, the sun striking the rocks fiercely. In the distance, near the mountaintop when the noonday sun lights innumerable bonfires, there in the mountains you can see them always. At first you don't know who they are or the places your gaze rests on. Then you understand, you begin to make out the shapes. Mostly they are women, but sometimes you spot the body of a child bent over the sand.

You return to Calama* and ask about what you have seen in the hills, and they tell you they are the widows of Calama. One day like any other, soldiers came for the young men who worked in the factory in town. The soldiers promised they would come back, but they took the men away with their hands tied. Suddenly, on the same hill where you see the women, the men are killed, shot in the back by these cowards.

The widows do not stop searching for them, every day, regardless of the sun beating down on them, and they search for the bodies, the remains of their bodies, with tiny bird feathers. And so they comb the sand for whatever they might find—tiny bits of fingernails, hair. That is what the women do in the sand, their search never-ending, as is their sorrow.

---

*Calama is a mining town in the north of Chile. The military government committed a horrible crime when it murdered more than fifteen young men in the hills outside the city. The man responsible for this was Colonel Arellano Stark, and he later confessed to this crime. The story of the widows is true, and they continue to search for the remains until today. This event took place in 1988.

A Note in an Open Book

When did we stop being lucid in our dreams? When did we decide to be levelheaded? At what moment did we abandon hope, and what happened when we left? Did we leave the windows half-open in order to imagine the first rains, the frost on a window shattered by the winds? Did someone leave a note resting on a poem in an open book?

We left too soon, and life, dreams, and the hope of being young were taken from us. The dictatorship robbed us of our youth, our passion, the discovery of mad genealogies that had more to do with the flavor and lore of the soul. And so we became ever darker, more cautious, stern, and crushed by what was not said. Forever repeating that dream of the night, we fled the house where no one slept and were transformed into informers.

Suddenly night fell, a long night, and we were left alone with the moon and our memory.

Cartagena

In Cartagena every summer the ladies of the ocean return with their parasols the color of sand and their faces split by the sands. Their gazes are remote, like the foreign women who gaze vaguely at an alien horizon. They gaze at the others on the beach with the clear body of desire, and perhaps they see themselves in other times, when the warm wind became entangled in their legs and the sea algae sported with their nakedness.

Now they recognize only each other, and the others watch them with the disdain we show toward abandoned objects. They maintain distant murmurs, and perhaps memory transports them to the diaphanous ambiguity of love.

In Cartagena the women dream of caresses, what lies beyond the horizon that surrounds them, and every year they repeat that act of returning together to the sea to listen to its hoarse voice, its anxious melody, its restless sorrow.

Now Cartagena is a dilapidated resort. Before, it had its moments of glory when the women with wide-brimmed hats and imported fans would strut along the immense seawall that now lies forgotten by poverty and time. I always loved this place for its glorious past submerged in the chiaroscuro of history. The women who still live there retain the beauty of those former days and carry an elegant palace in their souls.

This is what the sea was—privilege of recognition, knowledge of a gaze over a movement that demands hypnotic patience, the privilege of faith that is movement, cadence, an eruption of secrets. And so beside the sea I let myself be transported by the inexact plenitude of time, guiding myself by the rhythm, the sound, what the wave brings back, what the wave takes away.

Women in My Mind

It is nostalgia for the women of the house, the ones who chat with sprouting bay leaves and distribute sprigs of rosemary. I imagine them reclining on an afternoon, ignoring time and their fragile calendars. They are guided only by the Three Marys or the Southern Cross, perhaps by the warbling of a bird that announces guests, the premature arrival of a winter in its nightshirt of misty frosts, or the arrival of a distant lover amid the hoarfrost.

I see them always, or rather, they reveal themselves to me, guarding my steps as they did in the astonishing awkwardness of childhood. I sat beside them and learned the magic of shelling peas one by one, as if I were opening the heart of things, as if my hand were a palm leaf navigating along the seams of the earth.

I long for the women of the house with their tongues of stone or wool and their smiles like the crystalline water of those rivers that rise in the south of the world where innocence still awakens in the mornings and bread rises firm and fair on everyone's table. Nostalgia for the women of the house and for that love devoid of interests, simply gratitude for the time and the light, their hands, like fireflies, poured over mine.

·:· Part III ·:·
Exile and Return

Prelude III
The Beginning of Exile

A million Chileans left their country as exiles, and I too with my family formed part of this story of refugees and nomads. This final section of the book recreates those harsh years of the military dictatorship as the time of exile. They were difficult times, but at the same time, they managed to show the best of the Chilean people who valiantly struggled against those dark days.

Exile means existing and not existing, living between worlds, dreaming of the south and living in the north, being dislocated, always speaking with an accent, and missing being recognized in your mother tongue, the first one, the happy one, the original one.

My exile coincides with the political history of Chile. My father, a great professor of medicine and biochemistry, refused to live in a dictatorship. We were not forced to flee, but exile became a choice for us. I have lived outside of Chile since 1971, but I have always returned to Chile, even during the most violent periods of the dictatorship. My life has been a constant coming and going between Chile and the United States, and sometimes between Europe and the United States. I do not feel forced to live far from my country, since I have always been able to return to it, and I have been able to dream it and preserve it through the words I write in a notebook, remembering the sorrow of distant dreams.

This section has a spirit that fluctuates between past and present, covering the time from 1971 until the present.

The Footsteps of Clamor

Years of fear taught me to live slowly and deliberately. Invisible things acquired luminosity. I understood the murmur of leaves and the clamor of birds. I lived alone in a room that defied darkness. I learned to hear what is almost a silent language, objects from a secret age.

When I left Chile I visited the grave of my grandmother to say goodbye to her and ask her light to accompany me. Thus, I was also born with a suitcase under my arm, and I set about searching for some place that might be good for Jews. I arrived in North America, where I learned what total isolation was, in spite of a world of constant smiles, of calendars filled with superfluous events. I lived there hoping to return, knowing full well that nothing I had left behind that October morning would be there at my side.

Nights of Exile

Sometimes I imagined night in my country on those days when absence seemed to gnaw away at my days. I imagined night arriving like a lark, night falling in every season, especially in summer when you could recognize the rhythm of objects by their fragrances. From the balcony of my grandmother's house, I would stare at the drooping honeysuckle, the jasmine. I would stare at the benches in the plazas where lovers played with fireflies and desire. I loved the night that seemed at times to be a panting heart and, other times, a heart in love.

I liked the night in order to sit with my arms naked and a light shawl covering my shoulders. I felt protected by the delicacy of this light fabric that made me understand the impermanence of objects, the fragility of the passing of time. But at the same time, night seemed to be a queen to me, a pathway of routes, a fountain in the midst of darkness.

Sometimes I loved the winter nights when I would go out on the balcony to make certain of the darkness beating inside me, a darkness that also imagined the light coming after night. I went out to savor the smell of burning logs, roasted chestnuts, of lovers woven together, one hand over the other, like the beginning of trees planted nearby that recognize each other.

I loved the night because the women in our house told me this was the moment to invent fables, and they would sit in the garden in the light of white candles to conjure up the story of the disappeared, nocturnal witches perpetually navigating through southern seas.

In exile I fled from the night. And exile was not only a word bound to nostalgia, it was a profound grief, like an iceberg sailing through our souls and freezing our bodies. I returned to closed rooms, silenced hotels, the silence of strangers in rooms without a balcony, without memory. Then in order to sleep I would conjure up the arrival of night and dream about the stars of the Southern Hemisphere or simply devote myself to holding a conversation with God.

Exile marks us like a talisman or a tattoo. It teaches us how to endure long nights and short days.

My Own September 11th

Often we ask ourselves, how should we commemorate history? Shall we create private ceremonies in the isolation of our homes? Should we go out on the anniversaries of wars and victories to march among the multitudes to thus mitigate our alienation?

Each September 11, my family remembered Chile with a heartbreaking silence, a silence deep as a moan. Memory did not turn to landscapes or people or the moment when we left our country. Perhaps the uniqueness of memory is too painful. Memory becomes narrow, it does not manage to grasp with absolute certainty all sense of ambiguity, it becomes distorted. Nevertheless, we remember without question the radiant morning of that September 11 covered with smoke, or the word of a president whose tenuous voice seemed to whisper and assure us that it was still possible and necessary to believe in and defend joy and hope.

Our memories were rather a nostalgia that slipped through the senses, a nostalgia that affected the body in its totality, the palate, the fragrances, the Spanish language I carried with me and which is perhaps the pillar of memory that refuses to abandon me. I still write in Spanish, the language of my affections.

Sometimes my mother used to say that our life in that country at the end of the earth, a country like a balcony overlooking the sea, would be peaceful, with traditional family meals, weddings, and funerals. I would gaze at her in silence and not dare to tell her that that almost paradisiacal illusion of what the homeland was might be a misunderstanding, one more chimera to which the exiled frequently return, to live through nostalgia, to imagine the homeland in the distances, knowing full well that returns are always impossible.

I always thought that if we had remained in Chile and lived under a dictatorship, I would not be alive, or perhaps, I would be half-alive, because it is impossible to live completely and fully after being tortured. The best speculations were left to fate. The fact that we were destined to live in North America is a paradox. The "Colossus of the North," as the Nicaraguan poet Rubén Darío characterized it in the nineteenth century, is responsible for the military coup in Chile, for the conspiracy and betrayal of a democracy. The words of Henry Kissinger, who said publicly that it was not worthwhile for a country to become communist simply because of the irresponsibility of its citizens, still thunder in my ears.

The distance and time elapsed over these thirty years have helped me forget the anger and aggressiveness I felt so many times on hearing this. Perhaps humor has sweetened my existence outside of Chile, and when I hear Kissinger's words, I smile. Chile was not an irresponsible country. It voted democratically for a Marxist president. Irresponsibility reveals itself in what happens in the United States, where very few vote, and the apathy of the citizenry becomes dangerous. In Chile, voting was a privilege, a joyful holiday. We were an obedient and exemplary country in our civic responsibilities, nothing like the words of Dr. Kissinger.

Unfortunately, I could not vote in the elections in my country. That was another story of destiny, and paradoxically, I managed to vote for the first time in the United States in an elementary school in the town of Athens, Georgia, our first place of residence.

In September of 2003, the ritual of remembering was different. I remembered the 9/11 anniversary of the United States, sensing a repetition of history. I have lived only for memory throughout these long years that sometimes seem to be a bolt of lightning or a story hidden in shadows. The night of September 11 commemorated thirty years since the overthrow of Allende, his suicide, and the complicity of our Chilean people, its army consisting of the solidarity of many and the indifference of many others. The entire world created memorials and paid homage to

Allende in Chile. I could imagine thousands of people in Europe and Asia marching solemnly and silently to pay tribute to the deceased president who today, even after thirty years, occupies a symbolic space of extraordinary importance, especially for the younger generations, for the future of so many who are ignorant of their history. I also recall that at the end of the eighties, the survival of Chile was celebrated with a convocation of Chilean artists who traveled to Spain to share the complete story of a censored and marginalized art.

That night of the eleventh, I stayed at home, calm. I did not talk about this anniversary with my children; rather, I preferred to maintain a silence, a deep calmness on this day, perhaps to preserve memory. I did not go out to the garden as I usually do to name the stars, because I had that clear certainty that they were not those of the Southern Hemisphere, and that no firmament could grant me the peace or happiness I feel when gazing at the Southern Cross, the Three Marys, or the Three Pascualas, and that any gaze would be that of an outsider.

That night, I remembered what was so special about my country. The fragrance of night falling slowly, the darkness that was not uncomfortable or forced, and I remembered my mother's courtships that I sometimes confused with my own. That aroma of chestnuts, the night owls strolling peacefully because Chile was a peaceful country with a decent citizenry, which later became taciturn, grieving, and more and more introspective, deliberately asleep, afraid of itself and distrustful of others.

I thought about that month of September, when the forsythia with its exuberant yellow blossoms threatened to burst forth in beauty, and September 11 seemed full of the promise of life and spring, and that is how I spent that night of the eleventh of September 2003 when, in my adopted country, they remembered that other September, of 2001, the dead in the World Trade Center and the Pentagon. The broadcasters repeated the same things, they interviewed television personalities, Larry King, but never in the mass media was there a single recounting of my eleventh, the eleventh belonging to poor Latin Americans, Chileans, and Salvador Allende, who defied North American capitalism and who, simply for dreaming, were punished with the deaths of more than three thousand: disappeared, tortured, mothers in search of children, and widows.

The aggressor was not a faceless terrorist group. It was the government of the United States, the CIA, the administration, Nixon and Kissinger, sought today for crimes against humanity. And this is the reason why I meditate and write these pages, because in spite of not wanting to remember too much on that September 11 of 2003, I have dedicated my entire life as a human being, mother, poet, teacher, and activist to remembering Chile, to understanding its hybrid nature, its complexity and its innocence. And this long night of September 11, I felt a collective nostalgia for the thousand days of Chile's socialist government, a thousand diaphanous days, light and dark days. Days which I did not experience, being still a child, but classmates in upper grades told of their journeys to the most remote confines of the country to teach reading, literacy, and I listened and dreamed and imagined myself also teaching poetry in rural schools, and I lived those thousand days through the stories of others.

Our innocence was not only a childish dream; rather, it defined us as adolescents in a generation that produced many things—artisans' books, poetry, thousands of stories or thousands of days that became filled, were displaced, became joyful and part of our history. I remember that love was lived in the fresh air of the meadows, on Santa Lucia Hill where lovers kissed in broad daylight. Everything seemed to go beyond the body, beyond language, and life erupted in perpetual transparency.

The thousand days of Allende came to an end. But the end was dignified and silent. It had nothing to do with the clamorous noises of the generals or the perfidious and crafty look of Pinochet, addicted to betrayal, horror, and the perverse distortion of history. Suddenly, all of Santiago that always flourished with subtlety and, at the same time, strength became pale. Columns of smoke surrounded the city, corpses floated silently along the Mapuche River that crosses our city. Before, the fog was a sign of desire that surrounded the city as if it were a city in love. Now it is a wall that does not let us see either our past or our future. Sirens howl throughout the city, and children playing on seesaws seem to stop for a last moment as if they could foretell the future.

I will not dwell on the seventeen years of Pinochet in a country that previously gazed out at the sea and now withdraws into itself. It is ironic that during the Pinochet dictatorship, the history of the Chilean people was virtually ignored in the United States, the country whose government, headed by Richard Nixon, actively supported the coup. Most North Americans contemplate the history of Chile and the overthrow of Allende with the same indifference shown to news of other places where the United States intervened with impunity. They sit in front of their televisions, comfortably drinking Coca-Cola and eating popcorn, passively contemplating the horror of others.

Chile was a country with a long democratic tradition, an example for the West, with a middle class that knew its rights, a country with a long history of civil liberty and solid principles, a country that did not know the violence of the military, torture, or impunity, a country that voted with joy and respect. All that vanished on September 11, 1973. But Chile did not say it was at war with the United States, nor did it desire vengeance. It was a humble country, poor, without weapons. We remained silent and waited seventeen years until, again, in a peaceful manner, democracy returned, we managed to vote. Pinochet was arrested in London in 1998, and his betrayal was exposed, even though he was not punished for crimes against humanity. On the contrary, for humanitarian reasons, that torturer of young people, mothers, students, and workers was pardoned. He was entitled to a pardon and the freedom he denied to thousands.

My life in exile took place in the United States. In these last thirty years, I have managed to temper, with the peace that comes with distance, the way I felt. In those years, sometimes memory joined with other memories that were hidden. Sometimes it is impossible to distinguish the days of the years or the passing of one story into another. I think that perhaps we live always thinking about our return or, perhaps, our leaving, what we left behind, how we left it, how we had the strength to decide what we would take with us. But more than anything, I remember that feeling of foreignness that was my constant companion. I was nothing and no one. I did not belong to the neighborhood, the block, or its smells. We experienced days of borrowed items, waiting for letters and sending letters, and became accustomed to explaining who we were, why we had come, when we would return. No one knew where Chile was. The geography of North Americans was neither innocent nor ignorant; they were simply unaware of the presence of other countries in the Americas. They considered themselves owners and rulers of the history that took away our lives and identities, and especially our dignity and confidence.

Since 1971, when I turned sixteen, Chile has been my axis and my center. The country became the soul, persona, and locus of my intellectual activity. I read everything about it, from the presence of the first indigenous communities, its existence as a colony, its modern poets. I devoted myself to studying my home-land, and with the passing of time it gave me my career and my profession that is more than a trade. It is my passion. Chile turned into my own story; as an academic, I studied it, meditated on its vicissitudes, studied its forgotten women writers, wrote an entire book about Pablo Neruda, but I was unable to separate myself from the love of what I studied. I crossed the zones of subjectivity and history. I was not an observer at a distance. I began to be what I loved; I tossed aside the tenuous ties of academic objectiv-ity and combined thought with emotion, love of Chile with love for what I was studying.

During the decade of the seventies, at the height of the dic-tatorship, I spent several summers in my country as a student armed with books, notebooks, and tape recorder. I wanted to understand the dimension of silence, the face of horror, the tenac-ity of fear and hope. I met mothers of the disappeared who never feared the truth. To challenge the dictatorship, they embroidered tapestries called *arpilleras* that recounted the small as well as the large stories of the truncated lives of the disappeared in a country in flames. I lived with them during each one of these returns, and just as they embroidered their story with the threads of their truths, I chose to embroider stories—theirs, as well as my own—by means of words.

Violeta Morales

And there you are, in my mind, Violeta,* in Patio 29, returning when winter announces itself to you right in front of your eyes and falls and falls like a torrent over your always trembling hands, and your eyes, Violeta, become ever darker. Then you lean over the earth. You become one with the ivy, and it seems that your hands anoint the earth that takes shelter from the cold of winter, from the grief of time, your hands, Violeta. Always your hands that seem like a refuge to me, a spring of clear waters.

My dear Violeta, are you searching for your brother Newton or Doris's son in Patio 29? I see you, Violeta, in every season, always dressed in darkness, with your worn-out shoes, your tired shoes that no longer dance, no longer laugh, and suddenly, Violeta, I reach you. I embrace you because the earth carries your name. It smells of you, Violeta, and even though we have not yet found them, we have found each other and continue our search, this meeting that is repeated in every geography. But we are here, Violeta, in this Patio 29, and we do not know whom we seek, but it is that tenacity, that desire, like the passion of stirring up the earth, like someone who stirs up the devoted silence, the chained walls, and finds herself with the smell of jasmines and perhaps Newton or Doris's son, but you and I, Violeta, have made a pact in this cemetery, and I have found you among the jasmines, and your eyes, Violeta, wear the color of your name, of the horizon.

---

*Founding member of the organization of families of the detained and disappeared in Chile, a human rights organization that seeks those who disappeared during the military dictatorship.

The Body

How does the body of the tortured one love? How does it choose the rhythms of memory and oblivion? In what boundary of darkness does it touch the crevices of light? So, so many of them, of us, with fissures in our gazes. Hidden, distant, submitted to the silence of history and its perversities. So, so many of my generation were tortured. They were robbed of their bodies, their memories. They demanded names and more names, address books they did not possess, and they, so alone, howled alone in the remoteness of torture where torturers and victims alike took communion in the ceremonies of darkness. Suddenly a rhythm was reached, the time of rest when pain was mistaken for peace, anger for peace, and there were no desires for vengeance, not even for freedom, only to dream as in the beginning; things of the beginning and of peace, everything and nothing lay together in the body of the tortured one. All and nothing, beauty and hate. Silence and the word. Rancor and forgiveness.

No one told me all of this, but I managed to find out, to sense it, when suddenly dialogue turned into silence and I did not recognize myself among them.

Homeland

Was it worth leaving behind what we call homeland, country, history, language, and neighbors we fight with and then surprise by loving? I wonder why I left and why I am now in hotel rooms that accommodate my lack of identity, my need for my own home. I left to live in freedom, I repeat over and over. What price was that freedom? I live without being recognized, in stories without an identity. No one knows me or scolds me, and in vain I seek in others what has disappeared. Everything is emptiness. Long nights return to become even longer days.

Normality means recreating nostalgia. I do not know with certainty what day it is or in what world we live. Normality for others is the house where they have lived their entire lives, the Sabbath table, Grandmother's home in the country. I can no longer imagine any of that. We were always outsiders, and I still remember my father's taciturn gaze when he returned from certain towns where he journeyed as a traveling salesman and the peasants were afraid of him. No one knew him or had faith in him.

But I am losing the courage of my own faith. Living is sometimes too futile. I left my country, my classes at the university. The autonomy of pleasure and ambiguity does not exist. They closed the schools and life has become a commonplace, a series of banal phrases like, "It is good to live in orderliness."

At night I imagine moaning and howling, murmurs of tortured bodies. That is how I penetrate the nightmare of others that seems my own. That is why I left and why I am here and yet not here, feeling my way, learning what it means to be a foreigner, speaking briefly about the fate of a country too distant to interest others.

Frida Haase

I learned that permanence did not lie in the landscape or in the embers of the landscape but rather in the time of words, in their density or their lightness. Speech was my story and when I returned to the south, all the women sang the syllables like an alphabet I already knew.

Yesterday I wanted to see Frida Haase.* Everyone else from the area has died, even though people say that the dead grieve in the countryside. I wanted to get closer to her so she would tell me stories with her voice of a calm child. The hotel lies there like a dejected figure, a lady approaching the folded skirts of death. Frida Haase signals me from her window and asks me about things of the past, as if I had never left that place, as if that past I desire so much had never left my side. The past is a train that never arrives on time. My father at the end of the world and I thinking about the sunsets and the return of long nights. Frida Haase exists in the past and tells me stories.

* A well-known person who lives alone in an abandoned hotel in Port Octay. Her family is one of the many German settlers who populated the south of Chile from the nineteenth century on.

I Did Not Recognize Rain
in Other Languages

I did not recognize rain in other languages. I had no memory of it. It did not sing or moan as in the Southern Hemisphere. No one waited for it, no one longed for it. It rained soundlessly, or the sound was impossible to remember.

I did not know desire for the arrival of the rain, the blue idleness of lengthy days when the neighborhood women prepared offerings, tender sweets to celebrate the arrival of the rain when we were forbidden to attend school, to delight in the rain, a bunch of untamed stars freshly fallen from the sky and my mischievous mother dreaming on the balustrade.

When it rains here so far north of my other life, I return to the south, bidding farewell forever to the eternity of exile, and I return to the patio of my house. And the rain flowing along the balustrades is a rain without witnesses; only I know it. Simply feeling it seduces me; I imagine it like someone who hears the footsteps of beloved figures arriving barefoot, in the inebriation of the water that encompasses stories, wells, enchantments.

The water that drowns itself in my lips like a caress or a poem thrills me. In the distance, birds warning of other times, in the distance, the women of the house preparing sweet dishes to celebrate the days of rain, to ready themselves and bury their gaze within the mirrors, in the celebration of smoke, in the precipices of astonishment.

Rain like wonder, rain in the time of women leaning over the balustrades, awaiting the arrival of water over their dry lips.

I speak with the animals, anxious over the arrival of the first drops. I approach the lovers, bewitched by a sky like a dark fire ready to explode, and it rains at the end of the world.

I return to my country that is my heaven, a paradise without foreignness, a fulfilling return. Rain accumulates in the cracks in the roofs, slides almost carelessly, and in this loneliness that goes beyond my skin, I settle into the gashes of memory and imagine the bells along the coastlines that blend with the sea. And that is how I survive.

Imagining Thresholds

At night I used to imagine thresholds, fragile inner doorways, stories that came unbraided. Everywhere I encountered voices of solidarity, men and women who knew about my country and also knew how to cry with me. Like me, they believed in dreams to anchor life. As I traveled through Italy, France, or Spain, I discovered streets named Salvador Allende, and on the isle of Capri, where Neruda lived, people copied his poems not only to remember his death but above all to remember his life and his love on an island made for poetry.

My cello and I played in cities that maps left behind. Beneath a victorious moon that paid tribute to us, people presented us with fresh fruits, small lemons, colored wool, and always that wonderful applause that lasted an entire night or an entire lifetime. Suddenly, old women with their faces invested by the sun and the golden rains and men both strong and weak sang "The International," and I dreamed of the words of Salvador Allende, who said that someday we would march freely along these long and beautiful avenues. Today I am doing that. We are free in memory and recollection.

We return to those small hotels where people wait for us with baskets of lemons and fresh fruit, rose petals the color of the sea or a smile. No one judges us or punishes us. They only help us live.

A House beside the Sea

The dream turns toward the house, a memory both distant and near. A house beside the coasts where you can barely discern the ocean; then childhood taught me to imagine it forever, imagining wakes from afar. I felt it, roaring, secure, never imprisoned. The house is made of stones and tiles, but I love to feel the cold on my cheeks. I rest my face upon the stones, I rest my dreams. My sister and I share a bedroom. I like the cots; a sultan's curtain descends over the world, over the coasts. I never want to be separated from the sea, my sister, or the things I love.

I tell myself stories, I talk to myself and the others leave me alone. I imagine the sheet is an immense cobalt blue ocean, illuminated, never distant, and I am a poet. Words are like the folds of the waves, undulating, fleeting. But then they rest in the azure immensity of a night next to the sea.

I imagine Chile like a deep ocean with dancing anemones, sparrows overhead, and trout, wonderful dancers. I like to gaze at the stars reflected in the sea, adore and experience the night.

One day I returned to this house of stone and recognized myself in it; I buried my cheek in the rocks, and all my words exploded in a single wave. My room was empty, without cots, without windows, the sea had grown smaller, but I was the same, and I learned to recognize the signs of silence and oblivion. Nevertheless, I returned. No one was waiting for me, only the sea, the stone house, the landscape fixed in my memory, and I felt part of this land, just like the water pitcher, the rain, the stone.

The Big Island of Chiloé

I have returned to visit Chiloé* in the eighties. Here the women dialogue with the mist. At daybreak they sweep their streets with rosemary from Castile to frighten away the spirits that perch on the rooftops at night. And they watch them sleepily from the dangerous borders of the sky. I see them placing rue on the thresholds of the doorways, so everything will be properly protected, so the long night at land's end will be delicate in their dreams.

The island of Chiloé has more legends about it than any other site in Chile. From time immemorial it has had its own myths, like that of the ghost ship Caleuche, which appears at midnight with loud music and dancing ghosts. Spirits and women who levitate mysteriously populate the island.

In the mornings I watch them move slowly, as if they had just emerged from the spell of that very dream. I watch them and they watch me and we recognize each other, because recognition lies in being magical, believing in magic, insinuating ourselves between the spaces of heaven and earth that become knotted together in a perpetual secret.

The day transpires in the space of a fragile second, fog gives way to sun, the sun to fog, night to day, and the thresholds like swings, where dark and light birds enter to tell their stories.

There, in the remoteness of these islands, where each archipelago breaks off from the other, life passes like a mirror that foretells and bewitches.

*In the south of Chile.

Gabriela Mistral

I tried to understand the remoteness of your landscape as you traveled, a stranger in your very own land, and like you, I became a pilgrim to reach the spring of your mouth verse. I dressed in clay, in drab attire to reach the Elqui Valley where the sunlight filtered your skin. Your words and the birds recognized your somber footsteps.

Gabriela, I have come to you in the fog of a fertile dream, to your home among the stones like a silent scripture, and among the debris and the salamanders I see you, a child grown old, contemplating the flowering fig tree, resting your hand on the ancient scriptures, invoking your god, the one who taught you to drink the water from Aconcagua, to stitch the trousseau of the betrothed who awaits.

And in that poverty that was your grandeur I recognized you, Gabriela, I embroidered your history, and on the wrathful map of your poetry I managed to find you between the signs of water and wind. And as night fell I heard you drinking water from the Elqui, walking between the fig trees, returning, forever returning.

Someone said it was summer. The hummingbird appeared within the density of the sand and wrote on the trees the word *joy*. The birds announced your arrival, the sun settled on my neck, and glory sprouted over the days.

Delia Domínguez, Friend and Poet

Delia, you wait for us on your farm in Tacamó, where the herons and the ibises watch over the arrival of your visitors. And you never cease to tell us of your ghosts, your great-grandparents who were settlers, who watch you at every meal. And perhaps it is for that reason in these solitary and wrathful places where the rain dissolves the roads and women go mad from the cold that you are not alone. Your ghosts surround you, they give you remedies to alleviate sadness, and your great-grandparents guard the depth of your dreams.

Houses

Always the houses. Houses half-closed, houses half-opened. Houses where suddenly light, words, histories, all vanish. Houses where everything smells of asphyxiation, assaults. We leave them suspended in a fleeting memory, but at the same time, the obsession with the past does not leave us. Houses where we recall the boots, the methodical and precise stamping of heels. Houses where laughter is a flute, a waterfall, children who dance.

I begin the afternoons with a longing, a vague longing, fragrances, an afternoon stroll through Santiago. Here where no one strolls, here where no one emerges from these enormous mansions, here where no one knocks at the door, and if someone does, you are afraid to open it, or find yourself face to face with a beggar challenging the immensity of these houses. I imagine myself in my house that seemed like a ship because it was painted all in blue, and Mama said the color blue frightened away the flies.

I dream about that house where you turned my body into a seashell and we wanted nothing else and nothing was too much for us. We were happy at the level of our skin, at the level of a history it was unnecessary to recount because it was right there. And I told you about that house at the end of the world where Mama said that everything smelled like the houses of poor people, like coal and firewood, burnt flesh, and we laughed because we smelled of life, even our clothing smelled of life.

But suddenly that house remains in a mourning consisting of dried-up flowers and stories, a house where photos, jewelry, press clippings appear strewn about and everything seems like an echo that sketches other echoes. And the house knows it too, and bids me farewell, and suddenly I know there is no return possible for us, and I will never again hear the voice of my dead grandmother in the hallways.

The house, my house, abandoned passports, distorted signs, dubious smiles, and always, the knocking at midnight, fear like a profound rancor.

But suddenly I do not resign myself. I walk and think that I will be the house and the memory, I will be house, memory, history, my skin like a spiral shell, the voice of my dead grandmother dialoguing with my voice and everywhere, the house and I, and I seek nothing more than the present moment. And I do not accept furniture from well-meaning people, and I leave and I feel comfortable not knowing the exact address of my new house, and I lose all my luggage but suddenly I arrive at my own interior, the road that always finds its way, and someone has a face like a violin and mine is like a cello and the music opens up like an amber petal and I am in a square and my memory that has lost its memory is that present moment, the square, the moment, time, the surprise of having lost everything, the surprise of starting over again, the open house, peace, things that do not accumulate, the movement of air, like the music of the violin and cello.

The German School in Osorno

I return to Osorno with my friend Delia Domínguez, the poet, and experience wonderful days. People know me as the daughter of Frida Halpern whose parents were German. Chile hides things and returns them. I like Osorno. I imagined it as a phantom city with great secrets and women with the souls of foreigners. This is the province, the heart of it, a zone of mischievous and daring mists. My mother used to tell me stories. I imagined her face behind the balustrade gazing at the Canada geese.

I try in vain to return to a city that digresses in my memory and speaks to me through the voice of my mother. It is the only city I remember, and I cannot stop remembering it, in spite of the fact that I never lived there.

In the square everything stands still. The women are always dressed like dark clouds. Summer is shy and slow like footsteps in the province. Shops are small and smell like an age that does not become stagnant but whose motion lies in immutability. It is a timeless time where each day is like all the others and signs speak to us of the magnitude of memory. In Osorno darkness seems to hover over the day. The province is a time of darkness, and from the onset of summer the signs of winter appear.

History barely mentions the Jews who reached southern Chile with scanty luggage and the seed of a dream. Behind them lay Europe, ripped apart and dusty, a hopeless grave. I always understood this city as a home for refugees. For others, on the other hand, it was always the city of the settlers, those who arrived to colonize and civilize Chile. Little was spoken of this other history, of those who arrived lost and alone at the train stations where my grandfather went to greet them.

In Osorno they talk about the Germans from the meat-packing factories, but they do not talk about the Jews who arrived by night at the German club. Little or nothing is said of that. It seems that they arrived and were forgotten with the same speed. The city records its history in different ways, it chooses to remember some things and erase others.

The German school still stands in the middle of the square, in the center of the city, strutting like a peacock. In this country they have always privileged certain foreigners and forgotten about others. Although suddenly they were able to remember the settlers who arrived from exotic places, like the Yugoslavians in the province of Magallanes. The Jews were poor, helpless, and alone. It was difficult to remember them.

My mother tells her little stories with subtlety. She tells them bit by bit. Her memory is as fragile as her voice. From childhood they said she had a voice like a firefly that was extinguished slowly and approached things slowly. Sometimes everything about her seemed like the moaning of a small ghost town within her. My mother creates spaces in her speech; her memory tapers off and becomes full. She talks more about the beautiful things: the long nights, the mirrors that reflect stories, a dawn that bursts with violet wings.

I imagine my mother's house like Delia's, with a wood stove that seemed to create wreaths of smoke and emit a noise like the wild things of the countryside. Delia and I remember and dream, but our conversation turns to the rhythms of poetry, the objects of an invisible countryside, and certain stories that very distantly and very suddenly mother would dare to retell. Conversations in Osorno are slow, and memories selective. Conversations after meals are lengthy, the history of the settlers is always repeated, and there are little pauses for cautious laughter.

At night I imagine my mother. I dream about her rarely, because I always imagine her awake. I see her gazing at the herons, trying to detect the rhythm of things. I see her beside my grandmother, who seems to be dreaming about the passing of the ibises. Perhaps I sense that my desperate mother wishes to flee but does not know where to go, and she still has not seen the sea.

I attempt to reconcile my good memories with the bad. I see my uncle, dead, but with the voice of a child. He has come to visit me. Here in Osorno they say that the dead visit the living at opportune moments or when they wish to reveal hidden stories, unspoken things. Perhaps it is in this house made of wood and in this iron bed with down comforters that I am reconciled.

Patagonia

Patagonia is a night of absences, of sounds, of spaces, a prolonged night of darkness and light, and in these moments of solitude, the human voice also dies down like the silences of a wounded wind.

The glaciers appear slowly, as if fearful, surrounded by the light of the wind, by the enigma of their shadows over the cupolas.

They advance fearfully in the presence of their own grandeur to cast off the attire of all humility, and they invite us to witness the immobility of time, the grandeur of a memory inscribed in ice.

Then I become smaller. I bow in reverence. The wind resounds like a wounded violin. I am a fragment, a chrysalis of these immensities.

They appear with sonorous majesty, a silent majesty. The wind drives me mad, the voice of the wind that explodes in the presence of glaciers that are not shadows, that are not light, only the history of a blue age sinking in the face of immensity.

I recognize that I am small. I am also a bit of that blue. I reinvent myself totally, spread myself completely through the heart-rending extension of the ice.

The ice grows distant, comes closer, eternal surge among the cupolas of smoke.

In Aysén the unconquerable and eternal snow describes crossroads of every story. The snow, forever, with its tangled roaring, and suddenly the Simpson River appears, narrow, delicate, tempestuous, like the waist of a young girl in love with her own being. The Simpson River winds through the snowy valleys, rises above the cupolas, red like the wine from the nearby vineyards, and so we become drunk in the delirium that traverses all times, all sediments, and suddenly the lupines along the way. Purple, rose-colored lupines embellish the territory, the slopes of the mountain range, the Simpson River.

In Punta Arenas you must learn to listen to the delirium of the weather, its cadences, its sumptuous spaces. In Punta Arenas the wind envelops you completely, ruffles your hair, drives you mad with its roaring, its voice sometimes like squealing, other times like a song that even the dead can hear. Then it tells you that every night the inhabitants of Punta Arenas pray the wind will not steal the roofs from their homes. Once in the middle of summer the wind, wishing to play a mischievous and dirty trick, especially on the insomniacs, carried off the roofs of the houses. The drunks say that on that night a purple roof in the guise of a magic carpet went flying over Punta Arenas, the southernmost city in the world.

I loved returning to the long nights, to the skin that recognized that daring fragrance. I loved knowing I was in the countryside where light and memory abandon themselves to pleasure and the sensing of time without haste. The hours are memory, voice, history, or a silence braided from other stories. My body no longer falls silent; instead it recognizes the signs, the damp earth with bodies in love. I lean back over the long night to imagine my grandmother telling me stories about the comet, and something like furor invades my entire body. It is a desire that does not demand urgency, a desire for life, the forest, and the sparkling sea.

And night reveals another night, and on that night, heaven is a star made huge by smoke. I love that night within the night, imagined light after the darkness, the rhapsodies of footprints that the silence of night leaves us. And within that night I write, the moon is a landscape that rejoices in the dreams of others. Here in the long Patagonian night I insist upon your visiting me. Come here, to me, the flight trespassing through the air. Come here to the heart of a bewitching night. Come closer to feel the lucidity of the light. Here in Patagonia where night is the night of the end of the earth, where the maddened wind whirls pronouncing the name of poetry.

Night above night, above the night, night. I translate the darkness.

The Ambiguous Signs of Sand

The sand slips between your feet, wanting to plant within you the warmth of ambiguous footsteps, times of uncertain voyages.

You like to rest your body on it, warm and golden like the sense of your first young body, invincible, mischievous, and you recall the boldness of those days when everything was a daydream and memory.

You always dream and imagine the same sand on the beaches at land's end, sand of the south, sand of Isla Negra where once you saw a man walking slowly along the beach, contemplating every outline, every story of invisible objects.

You were a child and you knew, like the sorceresses, how to approach the root of dreams.

You asked him to draw you a bell. He told you it was enough to imagine its sound. You told him it was the sand. He gave you drops of amber disguised as a universe.

From that time on you journeyed confidently along all the world's coasts. The sand carried you toward cities of violent footprints, taught you to see what history erases. Suddenly, you saw in the sand six million Jews, the dead women of Bosnia, and you gave them back their names.

Now in this half century, you throb, you feel again the full heart of things. You love innocently.

I Imagine Returns

I imagine returns, I dream of returns. I see myself, troubled and cheerful, in the streets, I see myself like a lost paper streamer from my last birthday, as if suddenly my happiness and my history have been taken away, the rapture of joy, simple, hazy, delicate like the mimosas that stubbornly persist in blooming.

I imagine returns, a truncated childhood. My father's books, setting themselves on fire. All of us setting ourselves on fire out of fear in the middle of a vertiginous September that found us trapped in the nets of history.

But suddenly I imagine a day at the beach, a smooth young body preparing for desire. The smell of love is the smell of the sea. In the distance, girls older than I kiss the boys, covered by dark towels over the sands, but the sun just the same is able to disclose their forms, the insinuations of a body that loves and is always an illuminated lamp.

I will remember these details precisely, as if the great story were surrounded only by quotidian things, by the roots that suddenly become encrusted in our being, roots like trees, roots like mouths.

I imagine returns. I am another, and in another language. I have learned to translate myself, to hide myself, and only in the night that seems to be a blue lantern hanging from some mischievous tree, only there, and in that place alone, do I find myself, so that each night I return to the memory, to the pain of departure, to the fear of flight, of not being, like shoes misplaced in the north and south.

Tonight before I return I converse with my shadow that is my memory.

And Finally, Returning

I return without haste, do not fear the call for a truce. I simply return and it is the sea that grants me the gift of recognition. I am a sympathetic traveler. In my feet I preserve the secret of darkness and its alchemy, pathways of light. I return, I have been returning home forever, recognizing the wind that stirs the trees of the dead, and rush to the call of those who still wait in this generous land. I return by night, the sea dwells in the nape of my neck, hair swaying as if it were the wave where the algae rest. And in that desolate distance, in lands where no one called my name, I imagined the roaring of the sea, that vertiginous and husky sound, that sound that traps me to bury itself in its plenitude.

I have returned home, and on every balcony, I am the only one who can see the sea, the little bonfires of summer lovers, and more than anything else, those I love, Maria waiting in a rocking chair, Grandmother Josefina covered in her shawl, and all my friends, living and dead, singing the same melody. Happiness is a kiss from the waters that swirl around my feet.

Valparaíso

It is impossible to define this city with such a strange geography, where the hills are endless and envelop their inhabitants in a cloak of mystery and clouds. People in Valparaíso seem to live suspended between land and sea. Unusual events occur, like a bride running downhill with enormous high heels and a veil. The children shout, "There goes an angel dressed like a bride." That is why this city excites and enchants but also frightens.

At night the lights of Valparaíso were like an open book, like a braided jewel beside the surging waves. I have returned to Valparaíso like someone who returns in search of a former love, to recognize herself in the beginning of time and objects.

We stroll through Valparaíso and I still remember the names of the hills, Butterfly Hill, Englishmen's Hill. My mother used to stroll along Atkinson Promenade in mid-afternoon, at twilight, when the lights are fleeting fireflies, a cavity of stories, deep, and suddenly I recognize myself not in the precision of a geography or in the interstices of the landscapes, but in the burst of wind on my cheek, in the strings of a guitar that screams and sings. And when they ask me, What is the meaning of homeland? I find only these responses that are neither precise nor imprecise. Only the sense of voices that return after death or imagining a shawl of mallow wool. This is the meaning of homeland.

In the distance the dark and light origin of the coastline, the sound of the sea like a warning bell, like a poem full of fury. I make a toast to my parents and dead grandparents, who are buried beyond the hills. I make a toast to the disappeared of this country, who are everywhere. It seems to me that somehow Chile has been transformed into an enormous cemetery, and I approach the balcony of this little house with the face of a port and the heart of a handkerchief.

I name each of them, as I did when they were so far away. Now I have returned to care for my dead, water their graves, visit them on their anniversaries. What life did not allow me when they were alive, because of banishment, exile, and the shadow of loneliness, has been permitted now, in this life—to be with my dead.

I have returned to this country to feel the wind on my face and to get to know myself again, to smell my skin gnawed away by a generous sun. I have returned because southern signs have called me, and because, in spite of always being a foreigner, I am less so here than in other places.

At night the lights of Valparaíso lie on the threshold of the dreams of all the immigrants who reached shifting but secure lands with the angel of memory and his lantern of passions.

My Grandmother

During more than thirty years of imposed exile, uncertainty, and fragile rancor, I have returned to Chile, burdened with the enigma of a time that was not mine. Perhaps this will be the last time, to close up my grandmother's house. I was not with her during her last years of life, nor was I able to be with her on her dying days, when her body closed slowly like a secret seashell and prepared itself for the passing from one dream to another. I loved my grandmother with tenderness, compassion, and perhaps an incipient desire to know her better. Distance caused us to feel ever more separated from each other. My visits became more sporadic, and distance helped us to imagine the other as we wished she had been. My grandmother was a woman in love with transparency. She loved the rituals not prescribed by God but by men. All the acts of her faith were reduced to believing in the moment, the presence and fragrance of life itself.

Last night I slept in her empty house marked by the specter of death. I wanted more than anything to feel her breath, her laughter, her warm mouth, her false teeth that she left in a slippery glass. That night I dreamed of her with a satin blouse, a blouse she never wore because she preferred to cover her body with soft and simple flannels. Her nightgown floated over my forehead that was sweating in a sob. I was the old woman and she the young one who watched over my sleep and my awkwardness.

Very early in the morning I dreamed that the trunks of a forest had been transplanted here to my house in America. They were trunks without roots. I supposed the roots had remained in Chile.

When I closed the door of her house, I was overcome by a heart-rending absence. I felt that the earth had abandoned me, that I was an orphan as my parents had been in the past. I felt obliged to return to America as the daughter of foreigners, like a stranger in my own home, my garden that in the dream was a very dry pasture with all the dead trees.

Suddenly a gust of wind struck my cheek, the neighbor woman recognized me and spoke about my grandmother. In the distance I heard familiar voices. I thought that as I closed the door on Vergara Square, others had opened to me. I cried then as I had not done since childhood and remembered my grandmother Helena on her deathbed with her hands entwined and the Sabbath candlesticks preserving the mysteries of faith that were now mine.

Dresses

They still wear the gray dress of every season, a dress that does not change, a dress that sticks to the body, a dress like a downcast and dry tree. I meet them in the summer, but they are cold. Their worn-out shoes are a dry garden in the midst of the garden that is Santiago this summer. And they speak to me as in the slowness of a sob: the body has not appeared, the memory of that absent body, the body has not appeared, she tells me. Do you think they are cold? asks Anita, who has shriveled up. I listen to them, we wander the whole city, it seems to be a single threshold where we knock on doors that no one opens because no one wants to remember, because it is cold, because it is more comfortable to forget. They still wear the gray dress of every season; I move closer to them, and it seems like snow is falling on their hair.

Blouses Stuffed with Cotton

Some girls put cotton in their blouses and say it is a sin to look at their own bodies. I like mine, with its smell and its imperfections. I undress completely, on the very cold floor. I lean over toward the window so that I can feel the rain on my naked skin, and I celebrate my body. The rain is one melody, growing up is another. I sing the operettas my father hums. I am part German, another little bit Viennese, another small piece Chilean, and very Jewish, because everyone tells me so, and I find it strange that this seems to be so extraordinarily important to them.

I remember my first kiss, the slow and peaceful feeling that first kiss bestows, the tickling like an adventurous and fearful bell. The friction of the penis like a frightened bird that emerges and hides, that emerges victorious to return to its secret hiding place, my body, the other body, an exquisite and mischievous wing.

Sometimes happiness lay in imagining my city, understanding its curves, the crunching footsteps of mischievous children in its corners. Sometimes it was imagining the darkness, the house and its wood that creaked knowingly and always sensing the return to a house filled with stories and sorcery. When I was finally able to return, I had to flee again in order to feel at home in imagining my return.

I learned too many languages, and at the same time, to love in all of them, and perhaps in none, but later I discovered that love required only the gestures of a naked body the size of a planet and a bed like a small jungle surrounded by ombú trees and owls. From so much solitude I managed to learn the art of loving in a whisper and barefoot, testing the earth as if it were an arrival, a threshold and a fleeting paradise.

London

Pinochet returns from London. Justice has taken pity on his senility, but the mothers of the disappeared live only for the memory of the missing. Others grow accustomed to forgetting. Memory illuminates the darkness. Memory keeps us from experiencing the crevices of loneliness, even though the victims are the only ones who remember.

How can we live within these irreconcilable spaces? How can we dream about memory in order not to leave these events in the fissures of oblivion? Forgetting would be a betrayal of their memory. In the distance, always in the distance, I imagine hillsides and sobbing mothers with white kerchiefs, so that the image of those signals and signs will teach us to see the invisible part of that pain that seems to pierce the heart.

Pinochet disembarks from the plane, no longer in the wheelchair. Now he walks firmly like the soldier he always was. Many of his admirers applaud him. Then the same fear overcomes me again, the same questions descend upon me like turbulent waterfalls. Has this country changed? Why have I returned?

Osorno, January 2002

I returned to my mother's home to understand the story of her dreams, the subtlety of her progress, and the clamor of her silences. I went there like someone who goes in search of a former talisman.

The day is sunny and warm. Enormous pine trees surround the area, and the airport consists of a single runway. A loyal friend awaits me, the poet Delia Domínguez, who is from here. Her voice and her poetry rise in these solitary spaces populated by bold and untamed birds and smiling cows. She and my mother are contemporaries, but their stories are very different. She is the daughter of a distinguished judge and studied in a convent school with German nuns. My mother was the daughter of poor Jewish immigrants and was refused entry into the religious schools because she was not baptized.

My mother and Delia did not know each other in Chile. They met many years later through me and the poetry that unites us. In this summer in the Southern Hemisphere, when I feel so devoid of family, when it seems to me that I devote myself exclusively to celebrating the dead, they say I am a daughter of Osorno, that I am returning to my mother's city.

Today I return to her city without haste, but with caution. I wander through certain streets and certain hidden places where I do not expect to find anything but shadows, but from those shadows will arise a story without a present or a future, only a moment like the texture and appearance of dreams.

This return, this first sensing, makes me wonder about the meaning of homeland, and how we recognize beloved places. I am the daughter of that Jewish girl from Osorno who looked at beauty pageants from the sidelines because Jewish girls could not participate in them.

I notice that the word *Jew* is not used in Chile, because it is too uncomfortable. No one talks about what it means to be Jewish, and they prefer to substitute other, gentler, words, like *Hebrew*.

Port Octay, December 2002

Returning to the zone of shredded memory is inevitable. I return to the south and Port Octay. On the way the women are mirages translating the sparkle of light from the darkness. I want to return to Frida Haase's hotel to discover whether fear sets down roots there or if it is still a dark zone like the root of a disturbing dream.

There is Frida Haase's hotel, but it is an uninhabited hotel, with its twenty-one beds all made up, awaiting perhaps the arrival of the Prince of England, as happened more than forty years ago, so that Frida Haase can tell us this story, the only one she ever had and continues to have.

From the loneliness of the past that runs through the countryside, Frida Haase discovers herself. From her antique iron bed she gazes at herself, always inward, her hands two herons resting on her heart that seems to be a window toward the southern part of the world, the winds, and all objects. I approach her so she will recognize me and ask her to play the piano for me as she used to do in the solitude. Frida Haase rises like a captive or bewildered bird and goes outside dressed completely in tulles and crepe. The clock stops at midnight, and its sad bells toll. The piano is a distant sound, a fountain of dry water, and Frida Haase, somnambulant, sings.

Then I discover that you never lose your fear.

Happy Birthday, Pablo

I imagine planet Earth celebrating your birthday, Pablo. I imagine women and men reading your verses in Iraq, in Afghanistan, on the Bolivian high plain, but above all in Chile, where your poetry is a vigorous root, a root that shifts, conjures up stories. It caresses words and caresses all of us to combat loneliness, the intense sorrow of being a man, it happens that we too tire of being men, of being women, but poetry, your poetry was the throbbing of our senses, the dimension of happiness and sadness, everything, absolutely everything together, turned upside down in a simple wineglass made of clay.

Today we celebrate your one hundred years. The world salutes you and pays you homage. But they are not foolish tributes, they are not celebrations out of duty where the correct words, obedient words were calculated. We celebrate you because we love you, because we want you to know that on so many cold nights or on so many nights when passion filtered through like an incandescent moss on our skin, you were at our side. Because at times when we were torn apart, you were with us in the book that fell gently into our hands, with verses that opened our hearts.

Clouded Mirrors

The passing of time is a clouded mirror like the one my grand-mother Helena used to cover when she perceived the stealthy footsteps of death. Maps as well as chronologies remind me of the closed house of memory, a house of thresholds and silences, gazes of faith and fear. Sometimes it is enough for me to close my eyes to conjure up Grandmother's spirit, and she appears with her garnet bracelet and her gaze of a wise and mischievous fairy. She is on the balcony of her house, gazing at the palm tree. That palm tree still has not changed its verdure; it is infinite like the forests of southern Chile. It does not grow or shrink; it is a green-ish magenta braid of infinite permanence. That is why Helena, who wore her exile like a diadem that adorned her entire being, contemplated the palm tree, to ensure that days were days, and nights, nights, that the poppies were always red and beautiful.

The palm tree is still there at the house on the corner. Other people live in what was formerly the realm of my faith and imagi-nation. But sometimes on the precipices of insomnia, I sway to and fro, my hair blazes like a river of poppies, and I approach the palm tree. I see it as it was, with its bright green branches and noble trunk. At the same time, I imagine it very fragile and know it would take only the slightest motion of gentle winds to uproot it from the earth.

The palm tree is similar to our own history: tenacious in its desire to survive, fragile in its experiences on earth. A distant gust of air disturbs it, and, nevertheless, there it is with its voice that sometimes moans and sometimes sings, with its branches similar to garlands on festive days. I love it, and on nights of impenetrable loneliness, when I do not recognize myself or it, I feel its fluttering, its smoothness that overshadows sorrow and softens the cortex of the dream.

Transitory Spaces

Sometimes it is difficult for me to distinguish the passing of the years, and I recognize them by their absences, by cousins who marry, aunts and uncles who die, friends who disappeared while crossing the Andes Mountains trying to change their country and their history. I became a scribe who recorded only the stories I wished to remember. I wished to leave other memories in oblivion, but they always returned to me, to the interior of the dream and the void I always felt upon leaving Chile. It was a void that at night reminded me of the sound of a very dark piece of music or a nocturnal garden where it was practically impossible to find the road home.

My houses were only transitory places, and I myself a transitory resident in the middle of countries, cities, and towns. I never felt attached to any of them, only to that house on the Pacific Ocean that creaked in summer and winter, that only allowed us to hear the ocean in the distance, and where I let myself be carried along by the apprenticeship of memory.

I imagined conversations, pauses, and silences. The sleeping water awaited my returns, and I believe that is how I remained alive and awake, dreaming of returning to a country beneath the rubble, hidden behind a curtain of fog and fear.

Histories

The entire history of this country is divided into before and after the dictatorship. All the rest remains hidden, submerged among unspeakable stories in voids and gaps. One of them is Dignity Colony. Little is known about it, but on the other hand, a great deal is. It appears to have been a teahouse filled with all the sweets of Bavaria, but within it was a center of Nazi torture that Pinochet immediately decided to make his own.

Very few people escaped from it, but those who succeeded tell about its atrocities. The country is still incredulous. At first when people began to disappear, few believed it. At the end of this ghastly war, they began to recognize that this was a country populated by bones that had been torn apart, and an abundance of the dead.

Today people rarely speak of Dignity Colony. They continue to drink tea, and the only sounds heard are within our own consciences.

As in a Murmur

As in a murmur that disguises footsteps, I approach my nocturnal garden, tranquility rests in my gaze. I advance in the nakedness of a first innocence. The fog leads me toward flowers that emit strange scents in the night, omens that intoxicate, fireflies illuminating voyages in the distance.

I sink completely in the high grass. Someone is with me, or is it an anonymous shadow?

Perhaps I carry the dream of gardens. The sun has exhumed the earth to allow the passing of the moon, shining over the stones.

My steps, my hands, my gaze, do not lie in wait, they cease to exist. Earth is eternal in its beginnings. I walk feeling my way, followed by tutelary spirits, by the passion of a stranger who is welcomed in the gardens of night, and all around there is happiness, alchemy gilded over the darkness.

I do not know who I will find but I let myself be carried by the sinuosity of shadows that lengthen my path, the reflection of my body over imagined waters.

The nocturnal garden is revealed and it is mother-of-pearl dew wrapped in tears, scanty silence, crickets, phosphorescent lizards, smiling fireflies that pass and illuminate me.

Seated, I hope and do not hope. It is all a flowing of footsteps. At night things burst forth and reveal themselves to one who understands the magnitude of hoping. Silently I glide through a mesh of purple roses. This is paradise—a flash of lightning, an echo, night above summer, coasts.

Prague and Chile

Every night I experience the repetition of a dream that overflows the horizon of night. I see fields of reddish poppies like dark blood that assures the permanence of life or the outcome of death. The poppies are disorderly but always erect, and a rusty bicycle lies in the middle of this field of abandoned poppies.

Grandmother never spoke of the landscape of Europe. She only recalled the garden, the cherries in bloom, the unsociable neighbors who watched everything from the balustrade in the silence of the inexplicable, the silence of poetry.

The dream reveals itself to me after many years and ages beyond the shadows. I know the earth hides the crevices of horror. I know that in the fields of Chile, just as in those of Europe, are abject cemeteries filled with screaming faces and bones. In the first years of the dictatorship I came in search of bodies. I wanted bodies and names, I wanted addresses or simply to kill the enemy who was usually an innocent young man who had no other name but his own and for whom it was impossible to explore himself in that language that denounces.

The dream is what the poppies hide, what the abandoned bicycle suggests. Sometimes the dream is like a shadow of leaves and words, and I try to preserve that memory of someone passing through these fields or simply stopping in awe of that beauty. Perhaps the poppies are the flames of burned bodies demanding to be remembered.

The dream is static, as if it wished to leave a space and howl, but nothing enters the silence like poetry, like death.

Nostalgia

Years away from Chile did not relieve my nostalgia. Exile did not smooth the fissures of my soul, and that grief like a murmur carried within me is a gentle puff of air that at night seems like a ship that wandered and became hollow within me. Years passed that sometimes seemed like hours and other times like an eternity chiseled in stone.

I dreamed of returning. I talked of returning, knowing full well that nothing that belonged to me there remained. I sensed and then became certain that permanence must reside in the imagination or in a notebook where we jot down dreams. Sometimes I tried to remember my mother's face, passing my hand over her cheeks and forehead covered with rice powder, only to feel that everything was diluted with the fog or with the strange crackling of the rain that seemed to envelope me in an almost incomprehensible remoteness.

Exile resembled a state of mourning. It began to grow slowly inside me like a bold weed, and then it was diluted to return to the beginning of things, to the origin and lightness of history. On those rainy days I imagined the rain nourishing the graves so that those I left behind would feel less lonely in the loyalty of the earth and the absence in which I had left them.

Slowly the letters I longed for so much became more and more sporadic, telephone calls became more infrequent, and I was left alone with a memory that was at times slight and other times so sharp. On those long nights I contemplated my cello, the most faithful of all friends, resting in silence. Its belly seemed to emit strange sounds in the language of loneliness. Sometimes I held it next to me just to caress it and smell its wood that reminded me of forests my father described in Vienna, and I told him they grew in Chile also.

That is how I kept myself company in a country that was becoming more and more inhospitable and that forced me to tell where I was from in order to increase my sense of foreignness and invoke my past that was intimately tied to the past of the United States, but which everyone had erased and chosen to forget. I have come to believe that it is possible to select the zones of memory.

The Houses of Exile

Sometimes I wonder about the abandoned houses, houses left in the half light, the accumulation of secrets in them, what they wished to tell and what no one had time to hear. I wonder if they reproach me for my absence, if they too moan among the rubble and the mirrors that always reflect other faces and perhaps what we could not be or never were.

My house at the end of the world reproaches our departure. It knew how to welcome us without haste and was generous in its poverty. Now I do not remember the houses where I have lived. They all return to the heart of a story, the origin of the dream within these words. Suddenly we return to it, intact in our faith and a sense of belonging.

I do not remember the houses of exile; they all seem the same, with cracked walls and furniture the color of a cold night. I would lay my face on them, searching for names, familiar objects, the intensity of the air and stars. Today I return home, to the country where I lived, and I recognize myself among these objects, like the table where Grandmother recorded her sorrows and lit the candelabra at night.

When I finally return, I know that no one reproaches me, that everything is like a story still untold, and night is a red rose that will not lose its petals this time.

The years outside of Chile made me understand the rhythm of moderation. Each memory preserved in secret compartments occupied its secret and mysterious zones that reappeared according to its own rhythms and pauses. For many years I felt that life was breaking apart, swiftly or with a strange slowness where everything and nothing transpires, as if in one day we lived nights and eras in turmoil. Sometimes I would gaze at the braids of garlic that hung in front of the windows of the many houses where I lived. I began to understand that security derives from an irrational hope or from knowing that everything has its own time, its repose, its history.

I still cannot forgive the death of my best friend, who was so mischievous, so exuberant, and now, at the peak of his life, so dead, or reconcile myself to his absence. So many of my friends were innocent, pacifists, and they lost their lives. Everything I have written has been for the purpose of remembering them and not allowing them to fall into a shameful silence.

Saying Goodbye

Many times I imagined his death in a dark dungeon with enormous tarantulas, like the ones he ordered placed inside the bodies of so many women. I imagined his death in the Atacama Desert, where the dead trees were incapable of producing shade and the lips of so many prisoners never knew the taste of water on nights that seemed like burning days in the densest and most undeserving isolation.

My imagination did not foretell the death of this dictator, but fate or perhaps my own history caused me to be in Chile on the day he died. It was a transparent time, when happiness seemed like the wind, a harbinger of summer. I was with my mother and my cousins at a restaurant in a small fishing cove. The tables of weathered wood, the colored tablecloths, and a sublime guitar accompanied our lunch on this Sunday at the seaside.

When they announced his death on a worn-out television, the guitar quieted and I thought how it was because of this general that so many of us had abandoned the generosity of our ocean and the laughter of girlfriends joyfully descending the hills of Valparaíso. I thought also of the disappeared who would never return to life or to the justice they deserved.

The general did not die in a dungeon, nor did he leave so many mothers and widows in suspense for decades. His body did not disappear. The general died with a dignity he never granted his dead.

After lunch we returned to the city of Santiago. All along the way the silence was filled with reflection. The voices of broadcasters relived the fateful moments of the military coup of 1973, and contrary to what the world press was reporting about the people's protests, I felt that the country was hushed, calm, as if the specter of a dark cloud had disappeared.

While they kept a vigil over the body at the military school, and those who were faithful to the fascist regime bid farewell to their dubious leader, I imagined that all the eyes of the tortured, those mothers sunken in the deepest of sorrows, all the rivers of Chile where the bodies were dumped, would descend upon that amorphous body that could no longer respond in death, and that would never be judged in life.

Augusto Pinochet died on a sunny Sunday, the tenth of December—ironically, Human Rights Day. I think that justice can be seen in the humiliations this general suffered in his final years, in his arrest in London, and later in his house arrest. The only ones who carry within themselves the truth of what they suffered on those days when they were blindfolded and terrorized with torture, cannot speak, but it is the responsibility of a new generation of witnesses to write a new history of Chile, a country filled with heroes who are dead but not defeated, a country which dreamed a dream of equality in the decade of the seventies. I think that dream has not died, and the death of this general will inspire us to never submit to a fascist dictatorship, to always believe in utopias and the reality of dreams.

That afternoon I imagined myself again a young girl who went out to the streets to take pleasure in the world, in the smells, the fragrances, the possibilities of feeling filled with hope, and suddenly I knew that girl was still within me, she was alive and smiling.

I went out to the street with a red carnation and handed it to a stranger. Something told me that Chile was no longer divided. We are learning to live as a united country, and the death of the general has left us in peace.

I pray that time will help us to judge him, to understand that the search for the truth of those dark days is the true justice that each one of us is entitled to.

That night I slept in peace; the end of an era had arrived. At

dawn I opened the windows and gazed at the diaphanous cordillera. I said, "Good morning, Chile," as I always did until the
day I had to leave. But now I have returned. I remain. I am part
of this history, this balcony, this red carnation my neighbor has
given me.

The Illusion of a Firefly

Perhaps we did not know the revolving rhythm of time, the obligations that only promote rituals. Perhaps we thought the future was too uncertain, and our plans were reduced just to the transparency of the moment. We did not pursue great trophies. Nor did we pray in enormous concrete cathedrals. We pursued only the illusion of a firefly circling like a mischievous bride over the forests. We simply decided that life was worthwhile only according to the dimension of one's dreams and justice at every table.

They called us the disenchanted generation; we demonstrated political activism with poems under our arms and anointed ourselves with branches of dry leaves. We disappeared and even after death we learned it was possible to reconcile our dreams, freedom like a word with a voice made of water.

From my country I learned so much, above all to experience life, the air on my body, the rain on my cheeks, the paradise of the present.

Chile

I fall in love again with my country. I welcome it bless it curse it, my country with the name of a bird, with a body like a cinched waist. I recognize myself through my city, sketching sunbursts on its walls. I imagine it to be forever summer, pomegranates and peaches. The fruit vendor is the bearer of joy. I love daybreak, upon awakening, evenings, recognizing mornings, awakening, the sound of women sweeping the sidewalks. I return to it like a love both old and new. I dare to feel, to act, to speak, to caress, and to imagine. I love its generous coastlines, its rivers with names of abandoned princesses recovered.

I say *rain* and it is the sound of my homeland like a pounding ocean, a throbbing of litanies on tin roofs. I say rain and I seek the music of my childhood, afternoons in a blue house, Mama distant among the mirrors and the salamander stoves. I say rain and in the silence of a sleeping house water is a prayer among the springs of the sky. Facing the magnitude of sadness, we choose the magnitude of a smile.

I love to watch Matilde kneading the dough and Pepe inventing melodies on a homemade guitar of smooth and sinuous wood. I return to a country named Chile with eight hundred smoking volcanoes, poets prone to dancing, clowns for life, with my dead grandparents awaiting me on the hillsides along with Pablo Neruda dancing on Isla Negra as he awaits the returnees. I return. I will not leave here. I never left. Chile is the land of earth and sky.

About the Author

Marjorie Agosín is an award-winning poet and human rights activist. She has won numerous awards for her writing, among them the Gabriela Mistral Medal of Honor for lifetime achievement in the arts and the International Latino Book Award for her collection of poetry *The Angel of Memory*. Agosín has also written memoirs and essays. Her work has been translated into several languages. She is the Luella LaMer Slaner Professor of Latin American Studies at Wellesley College.

About the Translator

Roberta Gordenstein is Professor of Foreign Languages at Elms College in Chicopee, Massachusetts. She has published articles and reviews about Jewish and Latina writers in *Hispania*, *Monographic Review*, and *Letras Femeninas*. Her translations appear in *The House of Memory* (1999) and *Miriam's Daughters* (2001), short stories and poems by Jewish Latin American women, and the *Virginia Quarterly Review*. Besides her work in literary criticism and translation, Dr. Gordenstein has conducted teacher training workshops in Eastern Europe and Central America.

CPSIA information can be obtained at www.ICGtesting.com
Printed in the USA
LVOW06s0950130114

369128LV00004B/11/P